MW01119102

THE GOLDEN RULES OF RETIREMENT

A PSYCHOLOGIST'S GUIDE TO LIVING RETIREMENT TO THE FULLEST, NO MATTER YOUR FINANCIAL SITUATION

LEE PENN, PhD

Copyright © 2023 by Lee Penn, PhD, of *LifeCanBeGolden.com*

All rights reserved.

No portion of this book may be reproduced in any form without written permission from the publisher or author, except as permitted by U.S. copyright law.

Print ISBN: 9798860201736

Cover art was produced by the creative team at *Getcovers.com*.

CONTENTS

INTRODUCTION

What do the following events have in common: your first day on a new job, your wedding day, and the day you moved into a new home? For one thing, these are all major life changes. Mostly people associate such changes with excitement and hope for better things. At the same time, they are also sources of stress. Change and stress go hand-in-hand! Retirement also represents a major change in life, and so it is natural to feel stressed, lost, and overwhelmed from time to time. If you feel this way when thinking about retirement, then trust me when I say you are not alone. It turns out that retirement is a lot harder than most people bargained for! There are many reasons this is so.

First, we as human beings are creatures of habit. We spend ten, twenty, thirty, sometimes up to fifty or more years of our lives getting up for work in the morning. We get used to seeing the same people and relaxing on our days off. Our lives develop a rhythm, structured by the work week. Mornings I do this, 9-to-5 I do that, then I come home. To retire means giving up on the structure of working. It means we have much, much more time on our hands and no firm requirements to help shape that time. Suddenly we are our own masters with little to no experience in structuring our own time–how could we, when we've gotten into the habit of working so hard, pleasing our bosses or clients? When so much of our day has been decided for us? It makes sense that it would be challenging at first to adjust! Some describe the new freedom of retirement as like living on an alien planet. Others say it is a two-edged sword.

Second, finances can be a major stressor. For many, money has always been a huge source of stress, and retiring from full-time work can signal a major decrease in yearly income. Many retirees, in fact, choose to return to work in some capacity, and there is nothing wrong with that (it can even lead to a happier, healthier experience!). When we work, we give up our time and energy in exchange for income. Retirement in the traditional sense of the word means giving up money, but at the same time you get more time and save your energy for other things. It's a trade-off! That drop in income though, especially as prices always seem to be going up, can be a big shock.

Third, a large part of a person's personal identity comes from their profession (including homemakers!). Meet any new acquaintance, and one of the first questions after your name is what do you do for a living. For many in the United States, a job represents a sense of purpose and self-reliance. Even if the job is hard, we are paying the bills, taking care of our families, and making our way in this world. Talk to many retirees, and they'll share how important their work history has been and continues to be in shaping their sense of identity. Is it any wonder that people can begin to question who they really are after retiring from work? That they may begin to feel depressed, lonely, and insecure about the future?

Retirement, as with any major change in life, can be hard. But, it doesn't have to be! One of my mentors from when I was training to become a geropsychologist (a psychologist who trains especially to work with older individuals) had a saying that he liked to repeat: "Life saves its greatest challenges for when we are wise enough to face them." With the right knowledge, strategy, and plan, retirement can be the *good kind* of change. It can even be a golden opportunity for living out your dreams! It really all depends on how you use your time (easier said than done). This book is designed to help you tap into and generate wisdom for this exciting stage of life. By reading through the words and engaging in the exercises, you'll feel more prepared and be able to skip over most of the pitfalls that catch the average new retiree unawares. This is an excellent step, and I'm glad to assist you along this journey.

About Me

I am a doctor in counseling psychology with over a decade of experience providing counseling services to older clients. In order to achieve my degree, I had to complete a dissertation, which is basically an all-encompassing research project about a specific topic. I chose to focus on retirement planning due to the fact that so many new retirees suffer from increased rates of depression, anxiety, relationship conflict, and substance abuse. My hope was to find a way to help prevent such negative things from happening!

In the course of my research, I stumbled across a team studying much of the same thing. Adams and Rau in 2011 published a paper showing that not just financial concerns impact new retirees but also questions such as: "What am I going to do with my time?" "Who am I going to spend my time with?" and "Where am I going to live?" Using these questions as a guide, I surveyed over five hundred soon-to-be retirees about how prepared they feel for retirement and which psychological factors helped them to feel so. The results were very encouraging, and I was able to publish my findings in a top research journal within the field of counseling psychology. In short, the questions from Adams' and Rau's team were very helpful!

I have since used what I learned from my project to help thousands more retirees dealing with the transition into retirement. I do this by combining my research knowledge with exercises and planning strategies from life coaching, career counseling, and mental health therapy that have been proven to work. I distill this knowledge down into what I call "The Golden Rules" for Retirement, which are easy-to-remember summaries of research and clinical findings geared to help you succeed. I enjoy my career and am thrilled to see my clients meet their goals! Yet, I am only one person—the aim of this book is to share what I know in a broader way. If I can reach more people, share these helpful tools with a wider audience, then I will really feel that I have accomplished something worthwhile. I am glad that I can reach you in this way, and I hope you'll be able to gain some kernels of wisdom from the work between these pages.

But before we get into the nitty gritty of things, let's make sure we all have the same expectations. Let's talk about what this book is not, as well as what this book is.

What This Book Is Not

1. This book is not a guide to financial investing for retirement. There are many great resources out there on this topic, including books, YouTube videos, and financial advisors. They are qualified to help you invest and budget your money in ways I could never dream of. If you are looking for resources, consider asking the individual who does your taxes for a referral or ask a close friend to see if they know of any great financial planners.

2. This book is not a substitute for mental health therapy.

While there are great resources within these pages, I highly recommend seeking out a licensed therapist if you find yourself feeling more down or high-strung than usual or for a longer duration of time than is normal for you. Having a helper available who can provide feedback is invaluable. As well, mental health therapy can be helpful not just for negative experiences but also for identifying strengths and encouraging positive growth. You can look up therapists in your area on Psychologytoday.com. What's great about this resource is you can search for providers who specifically take your insurance, and many are open to meeting either in person or via computer or webcam depending on your needs. For those finding themselves in severe distress, I strongly encourage you to call the toll-free national suicide hotline by dialing 988. This 24/7 number is confidential and can be helpful no matter your level of distress.

3. This book is not an academic text. Although it is based on my research, it is not written to be weighed down by complicated theories, academic jargon, or lengthy citations of published articles. Claims made outside of the scope of my individual study are also backed by other research teams doing amazing things in the world. If you are interested in the research side of things, feel free to contact me! For those research teams and professional sources that I do directly reference, you can find citations at the end of this book.

4. This book is not a one-size-fits-all template for retirement. If you ask twenty different retirees what life is like for them, you will get twenty different answers. This is because the environment for retirees is constantly changing, and retirees'

needs are also evolving. The idea of working for a single company, retiring with a pension, and spending the rest of one's years free from work is becoming increasingly rare. Many, too, find such a life to be a bad fit! You are a unique person with unique interests and needs. Finding what works for you is the part of this process that can be the most challenging but also the most rewarding.

What This Book Is

1. This book is a source of information to help you get started, point you in the right direction, and develop a personalized plan that works for you with your needs.

2. This book is a holistic, or multi-angled, guide to thriving in retirement. While there are many books out there on financial planning, there are very few resources that address other important factors, like maintaining a healthy mood or taking advantage of the time available to develop a new passion. While money can help make problems go away, it doesn't buy happiness. This book is designed to help fill in the gaps.

3. This book is a collection of therapeutic exercises that have been proven to work for the most common issues that arise during retirement. You are invited to use your own paper for these exercises. If you prefer, I have created a free companion workbook that you can download and print out from my website, *LifeCanBeGolden.com*. To receive a free companion workbook you will just need to sign up for the Golden Rules email newsletter, of which you are welcome to unsubscribe at any time. I even hired a designer to make this workbook appealing to work with in hopes it will be helpful! If you

are interested, enter *LifeCanBeGolden.com* into your web browser and submit your email address into the sign-up box.

4. The end of each chapter features a check-in to track your mood and sense of self-confidence as you progress through the book. Hopefully, as you progress through the book, you will find that your mood and sense of confidence improve over time.

5. This book is your new support. Much like a cheerleader encourages the team to do their best, this book is here to keep you pushing in the right direction. At the same time, it is never the cheerleader who actually scores the points. It is up to you to engage in the exercises and put in the work!

6. This book is written primarily from the perspective of retirement within the United States. For this reason, there will be references to institutions primarily associated with retirees within the USA. For example, Social Security income is specific to the United States. Regardless, the general principles apply to all retirees. For information pertinent to other countries, you may want to reference online resources supported by your country's government.

7. This book is an *affordable* resource, written in *simplified* terms. Retirement is a challenge that we all will hopefully get to face, and yet I see so many good people fumble alone in the dark for lack of help. My goal is to reach a wide audience and help people, plain and simple.

8. This book is for anyone. Whether you are looking forward to retirement in the next few years, are thinking ahead to

retirement in the next few decades, or have already retired, there is information in these pages that you will find helpful. It is never too early or too late to improve your life. No matter at what stage you are at in the journey, you are taking an excellent step by reading this book! Let's continue strong together.

The Structure

This book is divided into different parts for two reasons: logic and ease of reference. Logically, this book will cover a wide range of golden rules that all individually pertain to successful retirement. Throughout these golden rules, there will be exercises that build upon one another such that by the end of the book you will have a personal, realistic, and achievable plan for enjoying your retirement. The golden rules covered will include:

Golden Rule 1: Understand Retirement

Golden Rule 2: Clarify Your Finances

Golden Rule 3: Healthy Life, Happy Life

Golden Rule 4: Get Your Home In Order

Golden Rule 5: Do Something Meaningful With Your Time

Golden Rule 6: Make a Plan

As we will see, the Golden Rules all relate to one another. For example, where we live will be somewhat determined by our financial situation, and vice versa. That being said, retirement is an ongoing, ever-changing process. My hope is that the above categories can facilitate easy reference for times in the future when you need more information about something specific. You don't have to deal with this huge change alone. Some have friends, some have family, but practically anyone can access this book. I'm glad that you're here with me. Let's get started!

Check-In #1

Here we have the first check-in to help see where you are at regarding your mood and sense of confidence for managing your retirement. The answers you select are for your personal benefit and need not be shared with others. On a scale of "0" to "10," you will select which number best describes your current mood with a "0" meaning "Not at all," a "5" meaning "half and half," and a "10" meaning "Completely." Feel free to choose a number in between the anchor points, such as a "6" or "7" to mean more so than not or a "3" or "4" to indicate less than half. You are welcome to write the number down or make a mental note to yourself–whatever works for you!

I feel down and worried when I think about retirement.

I am a _____ out of 10 at this time.

I feel confident in my ability to lead a happy and successful retirement life.

I am a _____ out of 10 at this time.

GOLDEN RULE 1: UNDERSTAND RETIREMENT

There used to be a very clear definition for retirement: a person reaches a certain age, typically 65 years old, and completely detaches from work. They then get to live out the "golden years" until the time to pass away. There are some more nuances, but that is the mold that most people fell into back in the twentieth century. Indeed that template is still the vision that most people bring to mind when they think of retirement!

In today's world, it is more difficult to come up with a single definition for retirement because there are so many unique circumstances. Some people leave work right at the age in which they will receive full retirement benefits, while others leave sooner than intended because of an unforeseen disability. Still other people never stop working or find new, "encore" careers. This all becomes more complicated due to the fact that people overall are living longer, meaning the stage of retirement also lasts much longer than ever before. Throw in the huge variety of things to do, sources of income, and places to live, and the possibilities for one's "retirement" become very complex indeed. For the purposes of this book, retirement will be defined as: *a new phase of life signaled both by a significant reduction in work hours and by the receipt of retirement income and benefits.*

Let's break this definition down into smaller parts in order to really understand what is happening here:

1. *It is a new phase of life.* While the line is vague, retirement represents a change. To some degree it is a subjective change, meaning it is up to the individual to say whether or not they are "retired" or not. Just because you leave a job does not mean you intend to stay out of the workforce; and so to be retired must be different from being unemployed because being unemployed involves the intention to find full-time work.

2. *It involves a reduction in work hours.* Many people choose to retire by quitting work completely. As well, a retired person can work a part-time job if they so desire, or stay on in their previous career field as a consultant! The important thing is that you are not working as much as you used to, gaining freetime as a result.

3. *You begin to draw on retirement income and benefits.* For many this means opting to draw on government retirement funds (for example Social Security Income in the United States). It can also include receiving monthly payouts from a pension or employer-sponsored annuity or drawing from personal investments (like a 401K or IRA account).

In this way, retirement means letting go of some or all of the responsibility and commitment involved with working. Instead of continuing to trade your time and energy for money, you now get to draw on money set aside and protected for retirement life. The equation "Time is money" is now reversed to "Money gives you time." And without a full-time job, retirees typically find themselves with a lot of time on their hands.

Retirement Today

Due to advances in medicine, people are living to older and older ages and spending more time in the retirement phase of life than prior generations ever did. As a result, there are more people at retirement age than there ever were before! Governments around the globe are working hard to accommodate this growing percentage of their populations while at the same time looking for creative ways to both pay for retirees' financial benefits and keep the national budget balanced. One solution gaining popularity is to raise the minimum age required for retirees to receive full retirement benefits. Whereas it used to be 65 years old to receive 100% social security benefits in the United States, now people on the cusp of retiring need to be 67 years old. Otherwise, they will only receive a percentage of the benefits due to them. And future generations will have to be even older than 67 years, as the age requirement rises for younger generations. For more information on your designated age for receiving full Social Security benefits, please reference the Social Security website at SSA.gov.

The typical retiree experiences initial "bumps in the road" as they transition out of work and into retirement life. Going from a structured work week to an unstructured amount of free time can be difficult for some. On top of that, citizens of the United States have to apply for new healthcare benefits in the form of Medicare and coordinate receipt of retirement benefits. Usually the budget for the household needs to be rebalanced due to changes in income. Filing taxes is different. People really start to miss their routines and old coworkers. Many have high expectations for retirement, and many feel that their real experience does not live up to what they hoped for. In fact, retirement can begin to feel more and more like a fulltime job.

The typical retiree faces more long-term challenges as time goes on, too, including declining health, increasing medical costs, and rising overall costs of living due to inflation. It becomes more difficult for some to see friends and family, and it begins to feel harder to establish new friendships. And, often people find themselves moving due to health changes and rising costs, adding on another layer of stress and headache. The challenges continue to mount: sometimes when health concerns become too much for your current living situation, residence in a nursing home becomes a greater possibility. Conversations about funeral arrangements and wills also become more common. It is easy to feel depressed, angry, and even regretful during these times.

I know the above seems like a lot of doom and gloom, but trust me when I say that things get better! Human beings are incredibly resilient—as a species we have made it through every challenge thrown our way so far. As well, hardships are always more manageable when we can see them coming from far away, can learn from the successes and mistakes of others, and can make a plan ahead of time. That's what this book is here for! In fact, let's take this opportunity to pause before we go any further and begin the first exercise, designed to help tap into your ability to adapt and increase your sense of self-confidence.

Exercise 1: Previous Successes

For this exercise, I'd like you to pull out a sheet of paper and a pen. Yes, you read that correctly—a physical piece of paper! What we're going to do is draw a line down the middle, dividing the paper into two equal parts. In the left column, we're going to give it the title of "Previous Successes." In the right column, we're going to assign the title: "Personal Strengths." As a reminder, you are also invited to download the free companion workbook from *LifeCanBeGolden.c om*—a free resource that makes this and all following exercises more convenient. All you need to do is submit your email address to the free Golden Rules Series newsletter, of which you are welcome to unsubscribe from at any time.

Once you have set up the format for the sheet of paper, we're going to start filling out the left column with brief descriptions of the challenges we've overcome in the past. These can be big challenges or small challenges, rewarding challenges or frustrating obstacles that you had no choice but to face. As you list out your previous successes—and they are successes because you are still here to tell the tale (in other words, you must have adapted because you survived!)--I encourage you to think back to that time in your life. What was so challenging about that situation? Were there any unexpected elements, things that you could not anticipate ahead of time? What helped you to be successful?

Now, for the right side of the paper, I'd like you to write down the personal strengths that helped you to be successful for each situation. It's important to focus on your own strengths and not others' for this exercise, as we're trying to highlight your own resiliency factors. For example, instead of saying: "My spouse's hard work" for this category, we can write down personal strengths of "Trusting others," "Teamwork," or "Maintaining positive relationships." Whereas the former places the focus on what your spouse can do, the latter three phrases are more focused on you. If you are looking for examples, consider the following list:

Personal Strengths: Adaptability, Authenticity, Balance, Caring, Caution, Creativity, Faith, Fitness, Flexibility, Focus, Friendliness, Generosity, Gratitude, Hard Work, Help-seeking, Humor, Intelligence, Kindness, Leadership, Level-headedness, Love, Open-mindedness, Optimism, Perseverance, Stability, Teamwork, Trust, Understanding

The list is by no means all-inclusive, yet it can help to begin generating ideas. Feel free to include as few or as many examples as you like, though make sure to have at least five. The challenges that most immediately come to mind are likely the best picks.

You may find the above exercise to be kind of silly, and that just goes to show that I can be kind of a silly psychologist sometimes. If the exercise feels uncomfortable, note that you do not need to show this sheet of paper to anyone. It is just for you! As well, you are just following along with what this silly psychologist is advising you to do, so you are off the hook. Reluctance or not, I strongly hope that you give it a try.

Hopefully, though, you can discover through this exercise that you have quite a bit of experience already with overcoming hardship and adjusting to new things! Retirement is an adjustment process unique in some ways, yet very similar in most ways to challenges you've overcome before. The same strengths that you brought to the table before will definitely help you here. Well done: you've already been preparing for retirement, even if you didn't realize it!

Let this record of previous successes be a source of confidence and strength for you as we move forward. This will be a good tool to reference at times when you feel discouraged, frustrated, or helpless. In fact, I recommend many of my clients to hang this sheet of paper up in a place where you can access it easily, like above your desk, on your refrigerator, or on your closet door. You have a lot to feel proud of already, and I want that to be at the forefront of your mind. You deserve to think positively about yourself!

Retirement Stories

Now let's take a look at other retirees who found themselves confronted with challenges common to retirement. Throughout this book we'll see their stories evolve and consider the solutions they settle upon. One of the most effective ways to learn and grow more confident is to follow the examples set by other people! As you read, consider what you might do if you found yourself in their situations.

Financial Phineas. Phineas and his spouse have always taken a hands-off approach to managing their finances. They were never irresponsible with their spending, and they always managed to cover their bills. But there always seemed to be another big expense on the horizon, and by the time Phineas became old enough to leave work and draw on retirement benefits he found he had very little saved. As he thought about his future he grew anxious and stressed. He feared that he and his spouse would become homeless.

Henrietta Health. Henrietta had always worked desk jobs: insurance sales, office manager, and a human resources representative. While not very physically demanding, she spent much of her workday seated. Plus, the stress could really build up! When the pressure grew intense she would turn to M&M's and Coca-Cola, her favorite snacks. In fact, she was always known around the office as the person who *loved* M&M's. At her recent annual health check-up, her PCP warned her that she was now pre-diabetic and would develop Type-2 Diabetes Mellitus if she did not change her diet and activity level. Henrietta hoped to retire soon, but now she feared that her days relaxing on the beach would be marred by finger pricks for sugar levels and insulin shots.

Residential Reginald. Reginald lived and worked in the same area of the country where he was born and raised. Life was good–there were friends always at hand, and he knew the area well. As time went on, though, his children moved away to other cities for school and work, and his friends seemed to slowly disappear, for one reason or another. Plus, things around town were getting so expensive! And it didn't help that he was starting to have trouble with the stairs in his home. His old stomping grounds just didn't feel the same. Soon he found himself isolating at home and feeling miserable. For the first time, he thought about moving to a new area. But, the thought of packing up all of his stuff and moving to a new place was overwhelming. He didn't know what to do, but he knew that something had to change.

Free-Time Felecia. Felecia was a self-proclaimed workaholic. She thrived in the office, putting in extra hours and strategizing about her next big project or work task. She shaped most of her identity and self-worth around her job, taking immense pride in the praise she received and the money she brought home... So it was an immense shock when she was suddenly laid off late into her career due to budget cuts. For the first time in years she found herself bored at home with nothing to do. She wondered if the rest of her life would feel this way: aimless, unstimulated, and resentful.

The above stories represent common issues that show up in the early days of retired life. That being said, there are many who thrive with the change, viewing retirement as a golden opportunity to live life in a more fulfilling way. Below are some true stories about people who made something great out of retirement. As you read, I encourage you to begin thinking about your own story. What would you like to be able to say when someone asks how retirement is going for you?

Retirement Revamped

- Mr. and Mrs. A discovered that many cruise lines now offer onboard medical care. As a result, they now spend more than half the year traveling the globe on their favorite cruise line.

- Ms. B spends her time fundraising for her church ministry. She solicits donations from her room in a nursing home, calling potential donors on her cell phone. If asked, she'll show you photographs of the churches she's helped to build in foreign countries.

- Mr. C worked as a long-distance trucker. He'd always loved music, and he would pass the time listening to his favorite songs on the radio. When the pressures of the road became too much for him, he picked up his guitar–he'd always fiddled with it when home–and began taking free lessons at his local college. Now he plays in an AC/DC cover band with his friends.

- Mrs. D always enjoyed working with children. When her husband retired, she helped renovate and sell their house then used the money to buy a duplex with her daughter. Now she's paid to be a live-in nanny for her grandchildren while her daughter and son-in-law are at work.

- Mr. E retired from the field of hospitality at the age where he would receive the maximum in retirement benefits. But, after a few months he grew bored and went back to work! Now he works part-time and leads training seminars for new hotel managers.

The list goes on and on, all the way through the alphabet and beyond. Just as there are many challenges that come with retirement, there are also many opportunities. There is no one right way to live one's life! Everyone has something in life that brings them joy. For some it's family, for others it's friends or good works or finding new experiences or something else entirely. We'll definitely want to prioritize such joyful things moving forward, as these are going to be the key ingredients for your happy retirement! This brings us to our next and final exercise for the chapter: beginning to set goals.

Exercise 2: Setting Goals

A goal is a desire that a person hopes to achieve in the future. Across research studies in Psychology, setting goals is consistently one of the most effective ways to take action. There are many reasons that putting one's hopes into words acts as a huge motivator. First, our hopes are often vague and undefined when they just exist in our heads. Putting them down onto paper helps to clarify what we want. Secondly, putting our goals out into the world acts as a reminder. The more that we verbally repeat our goals or read them from a piece of paper, the more we are forced to think about them. And the more that we think about them, the more we strategize, problem-solve, and work toward turning them into reality. Some of this process even happens when we're not consciously thinking about it!

So, let's take a major step toward shaping how we want retirement to be. Go ahead and grab a new sheet of paper and write down what your hopes or goals are for retirement. These will serve as your guide for the direction you want to go, and writing them down will help to keep you accountable. I encourage you to place them near where you placed your list of previous successes–somewhere of importance that you will see frequently.

When coming up with your goals, feel free at this stage to be as specific or nonspecific as you want. An example of a vague goal would be, "Spend time with my family," whereas an example of a highly specific goal would be, "Travel to Paris in the Spring of 2025." If your goals are vague, then that is fine as we are just in the brainstorming stage right now. We can refine them later as we progress through! Just get something down on paper. And, the more the goal is personally important to you, the better! One helpful exercise when brainstorming is to answer the following question for yourself: "If I look back over my life and X was not a part of it, then I would be disappointed." Whatever "X" is for you, let's make it into a goal.

The following are some examples of goals to help you get started:

Learn to play guitar

Take a Caribbean cruise

Research my family tree

Spend time with my children

Move to Portugal

Redecorate my home

See the national parks

Write a memoir

Go out to eat with my friends

Watch all my favorite movies

See a Broadway show

Run a 5K

Sell an art painting

Feel free to borrow or adapt any of the above goals. Try to think about both big goals and things you'd like to make part of your daily life. Remember, this is a list for you, and so we do not need to impress anybody else or even show another living soul. The important thing is that your goal will make *your* life better.

Check-In #2

Now that we have gone over the definition of retirement, it's time for our second check-in. On a scale of "0" to "10," you will select which number best describes your current mood with a "0" meaning "Not at all," a "5" meaning "half and half," and a "10" meaning "Completely." As you fill out the below questions, you may find that your scores improve, indicating less distress or more confidence. If so, then great! If your scores stay the same or even decline, then that is also understandable. Sometimes learning more and confronting a challenge can actually cause more stress! Creating a plan for retirement is a process, and we are just at the beginning–let's continue moving forward. With time, having a more realistic view of things will be helpful, and there is plenty of time for your confidence and mood to improve!

I feel down and worried when I think about retirement.

I am a _____ out of 10 at this time.

I feel confident in my ability to lead a happy and successful retirement life.

I am a _____ out of 10 at this time.

Summary

Well done! You are one step closer to making your retirement a success! We now understand retirement a little better and have begun to identify personal strengths and goals. Give yourself a pat on the shoulder (or hand if that feels easier) for doing a tough thing. Examining oneself and setting down goals takes effort, and so you deserve to reward yourself, even if just in a symbolic way. In the next chapter, we're going to be talking about the financial side of things. When you are ready, feel free to turn the page.

GOLDEN RULE 2: CLARIFY YOUR FINANCES

F inancial planning is one of the most common topics you will find when it comes to preparing for retirement. There are countless books, seminars, and experts out there ready to help. I will leave it to those more knowledgeable than I to provide specific advice on financial preparedness. As I stated in the introduction, this book seeks to fill in the gaps not covered by financial planning resources, and such gaps will be explored more in later chapters. But because money is such an important part of living in our society (It seems to make the world go 'round!), this book will cover general advice on financial preparedness. I've tried to include ways of thinking about money that any person in any financial situation would find helpful. All that follows is informed by economic theory. If you have specific questions or need direct guidance, I encourage you to speak with a financial planner. While it may cost some money upfront, such an expert can both save you money in the long run and help you to maintain your standard of living for longer in retirement.

Let's begin with a general exploration of budgeting.

Financial Budgeting

To start, we're going to simplify the complicated field of micro-economics down to two ideas. You have income, which is a category for all money entering your bank account each month, on average. You also have expenses, which describe all of the money going out of your bank account each month, on average. Money goes in, and money goes out–a song as old as time. You may have a large sum of money deposit into your account once or twice per year, depending on how your financial situation is set up. And, you may have large expenses that occur infrequently. But, if you average it all together, you can determine your general income and expenses. The general idea in retirement is for your income to be enough to pay for your expenses; otherwise, you will run out of money! In this way the same basic rules of income and expenses that applied while working also apply in retirement. But, the strategies we use may look a little different at this time of life. So, let's talk strategy.

I pose to you the following question: who is in better financial shape, Person A who has an income of $50,000 per year, or Person B who has an income of $100,000 per year?

The answer: it depends!

Talk to any financial planner, and they will agree that what you *make* is much less important than what you *spend*. How much we spend defines the minimum income needed to maintain the expenses of our current lifestyle. Or in other words, we don't need a million dollars; we just need enough income to cover our expenses! Let's re-examine the above question with some new information to help clarify this point:

Person A has a yearly income of $50,000 and yearly expenses of $25,000, while Person B has a yearly income of $100,000 and yearly expenses of $100,000. Who is in better financial shape?

The answer is Person A. While Person A makes only $50,000, he also only spends half ($25,000) of what he makes. This means that the half he doesn't spend can go into investments or an emergency fund. As well, if he were to experience a sudden rise in expenses or a sudden drop in income, then he would still be able to cover the bills, which are only $25,000. Person B on the other hand spends 100% of what he makes ($100,000 out of $100,000), meaning he has no wiggle room for rising expenses or a drop in income. Such a change one way or the other would be much more stressful, as it might mean he wouldn't be able to cover his $100,000 worth of bills! So even though Person A makes significantly less per year, he is much more prepared for major financial changes than Person B.

To highlight further the importance of expenses, let's take a look at another example.

Person A has a yearly income of $50,000 and yearly expenses of $25,000, while Person B has a yearly income of $100,000 and yearly expenses of $75,000. Who is in better financial shape?

The answer is still Person A. Even though both people spend $25,000 less than they make (i.e., $50,000 minus $25,000 equals $25,000; and $100,000 minus $75,000 equals $25,000), Person A is able to save away 50% of her total income while Person B is only able to save away 25% for a rainy day. In other words, Person A's income is actually enough to cover *two year's worth* of yearly expenses (i.e., $25,000 for year 1 and $25,000 for year 2). If her income stream were to suddenly end, she could pay the bills for another full year before running out of money. Person B on the other hand only has enough money left over to cover a third of the next year's expenses (i.e., $25,000 divided by $75,000 equals 33%). Person B would be much harder hit if her income stream were to end. Overall, higher expenses mean *your money won't last as long* and *you will spend through your money much faster.*

If you think about the above example in terms of contributions to retirement funds like 401K's and Roth IRA's, then every year Person A works, spends $25,000, and *saves $25,000* means one whole future year of expenses is covered. It takes Person B three years of savings just to cover one year of expenses (i.e., $25,000 plus $25,000 plus $25,000 equals $75,000). Person A could theoretically retire earlier as long as she kept her expenses the same. After ten years of working Person A could save up for ten years' worth of retirement expenses, while Person B could only save up for a little over three years' worth.

Now it is worth noting that the above examples are theoretical and do not take into account things like uncontrollable facts of life or standards of living. For example, one could argue that Person B has higher expenses because Person B is enjoying life more! Yet, this is not necessarily the case, as Person B may have higher expenses from debt, from living in an expensive part of the country, or from many other factors unrelated to living a "quality" life. We will talk more about re-ducing expenses as the chapter continues. The point is, it is important to consider your current expenses when approaching retirement, as these will be a big determining factor of how long your savings will last and how much your retirement income can support. It doesn't matter whether you have one million dollars or one thousand—if you have high expenses in proportion to your savings, then you will run out of money fast. In the end, it is your expenses that determine how much your money is worth! And, our ability to generate more income is much more limited in retirement (though not impossible!). We arguably have much more control over our expenses.

Many people don't realize how much money they actually spend from month to month. If that is you, then you're not alone! Others haven't tallied up their expenses for a long time and may be surprised at what has changed. This leads us to our next exercise: creating a budget.

Exercise 3: Creating a Budget

Regardless of your financial situation in the future, it is helpful to know what your current spending habits are. This will be your first sign to see if you will need to make changes moving forward, such as by reducing expenses and/or increasing income. Again, how much you spend determines how much your money is worth! Many people find that the act of calculating their budget actually helps them to reduce spending, so there are many reasons this exercise can be helpful! Grab a new sheet of paper, and tally up each of the following expenses as they apply to you. And, feel free to add your own personal expense categories if they are not listed here.

Hard Expenses. To begin, you will want to determine your "hard" expenses. These are bills that you must pay each month because of a contract of some kind. Examples include stable costs such as your monthly rent or mortgage. To determine how much you pay for each category, try to look back over the past three months and take the average expense total. Even just finding the "ballpark" total for each category is good information to have. Examples of "hard" expense categories include:

Rent/Mortgage

Car Payment

Car Insurance

Internet Bill

Cell Phone Bill

Health Insurance

Various Insurance Policies

Home Security Service

Pet or Childcare Services

Cable Bill

Monthly Subscriptions

The above represent the bedrock of your budget, as "hard" expenses must be paid each month unless you decide to cancel the contract. Arguably some expenses, such as for housing, are very difficult to avoid because all humans have basic needs. But others, such as subscription fees, cable, and even a car payment are not necessarily essential. In other words, you can cancel a subscription service but you likely can't live somewhere for free. Overall "hard" expenses are guaranteed each month–you can think of them as money already spent and non-negotiable unless you make a major change.

Soft Expenses. Next, you will want to determine your "soft" expenses, which are likely to fluctuate each month. These are costs that you still need to make to survive, yet they do not have a set payment amount, such as with a contract. Examples include your electric bill and your grocery costs. Because this grouping of expenses is not set in stone each month, we have some more control over how much we spend. Again, examine your credit card statements or receipts over the past three months and then take the average to determine your budget for each category. Below are some examples of "soft" expenses:

Water Bill

Electric Bill

Natural Gas Bill

Gas for Vehicles

Groceries

Medications

Pet Food

Again, we may have some months during which we run the air conditioning on full blast, while during others we may sit comfortably with the windows open. This is why it is important to determine a rough average. For those who are determined to never spend more than what is budgeted, adding on an extra 5-10% to each of these categories after calculating your total can provide a cushion against sudden increases in expense. This is also a good area to examine when considering cutting costs. For example, you can ask yourself: do I really need to buy name-brand items at the grocery store, or would generic serve me just as well? If I drive less or carpool, can I save some extra money?

Savings. Following, you'll want to consider future expenses for your budget, including payments you might make only once a year or in the case of an emergency. For instance, homeowners typically only pay their Homeowner's Association (HOA) fee once per year, while the need for a new roof can come out of nowhere. Both expenses can be pretty large, and both are much easier to manage if budgeted for ahead of time. Think about major expenses that you'll need to make for the future and consider how you can set aside money for them in advance. Sometimes we can calculate the average we've spent in previous years, such as adding up all of the receipts for medical bills. Other people like to budget for their health insurance deductible, knowing if they can afford to pay this then their health needs will be covered. The following are examples of savings categories:

HOA Fees

Healthcare Costs

Veterinarian Bills

Home Maintenance

Travel

Car Maintenance

Gifts for Friends/Family

Etcetera/Emergency Funds

It is a good practice to budget for emergency funds. When an unexpected bill comes out of nowhere or a tragedy happens, having this money set aside can significantly take the stress out of the situation. Financial advisors often recommend maintaining an emergency fund worth 2-6 months' worth of total expenses in order to avoid financial hardship. For instance, if your total monthly expenses are $2,000, then it is good to keep about $4,000 in reserve just in case. Easier said than done! As you use your budget over time, it can be helpful to think of your Etcetera category, too, as where you pull your money out when you go over budget in other categories. Just make sure to replenish what you "borrow" from yourself when you can.

Luxury. The last type of expense takes into account our "fun" money. Going out to eat, going to the movies, buying books–all of the things that we *want* but don't really *need* go into this expense grouping. It is important to prioritize leisure expenses, as our pleasures and hobbies are what make life so rich and enjoyable. At the same time, they must be a lower priority than the other types of expenses and should really be what we buy after hard, soft, and savings expenses are taken care of. Going to a nice restaurant is an excellent idea, but not if it makes it difficult to pay the rent.

Look back over the past three months and see how much you spent on fun things, on average. Common fun or "luxury" expense categories can include:

Restaurants

Coffee Shops

Movies

Books

Hobbies

Clothing

Entertainment Venues

Alcohol

Home Goods

The above lists are not all-inclusive and should definitely be customized according to your needs and personal circumstances. Knowing our spending habits from the recent past is highly predictive of how we will spend in the future, so this is a good place to start in determining how far your income will go in retirement. Let's take a look at an example now of someone who summarized their expenses using a budget worksheet. Remember Financial Phineas and his partner, who were stressed about being able to afford retirement? Let's take a look at part of his budget now:

Example: Financial Phineas

Monthly Hard Expenses

Mortgage: $2,000

Car Payments: $800

Car Insurances: $300

Internet: $50

Health Insurances: $600

Cell Phone: $160

Cable: $200

Total: $4,110

Phineas totaled up just his "Hard" expenses and immediately became stressed out. The bills he *had* to pay alone were more than he and his spouse would be drawing from Social Security income! "Dr. Penn," he complained, "Why are you making us do this? I don't feel better, I feel worse!"

That is a perfectly reasonable response to have, as finances are stressful to address! Part of this has to do with the perception many have that bills are outside of our control. We have to pay for housing and food, right? To some degree expenses are inevitable, yet as we will see below there is actually some control we do have over how much we spend from month to month.

But first, I want to stop and congratulate you. You have created your own summary of your finances, which is not an easy thing to do! Take a moment to pat yourself on the shoulder or hand because you deserve to be rewarded for your efforts. Looking at your expenses and tallying them up, does anything take you by surprise? Many people who do this exercise for the first time or update their tallying are taken aback by how much they actually spend in specific categories. But knowing where our cash is going is the first step toward making a change! I was shocked to discover how much each month my wife and I spend on our dog, Cooper. Between his special-diet food, his dental bones, his allergy shots, and his daycare bills (ironically, his daycare is literally called "The Pet *Country Club*"), our dog ends up costing quite a bit indeed. Throw in veterinarian visits and chew toys, and our dog is close to bankrupting us! But knowing this provides insight, and now we've been able to reduce each of our dog's expenses to a more reasonable level. If you find yourself surprised by an expense category, you certainly are not alone.

With your new expense sheet in hand, let's think about opportunities for making changes as we examine the next two sections on Income and Expenses.

Income

This is an exciting topic! Entering retirement means finally drawing on your hard-earned savings. All of that storing away, all of the hardships you've faced have led up to this point. The very act of working within an industrialized society entitles you to income benefits in your golden years in the form of government support (like Social Security in the United States) and/or disability support. If you have assets or savings, then all the better; but, having large sums of money is not a necessary requirement for a happy retirement.

To simplify things, we'll break up "income" into two categories: *passive* income and *active* income.

Passive Income. Passive income is money you receive from investments and government support. In other words, you do not *currently* work for it–you worked for it in the past and now get to draw from it. Common forms of passive income include Social Security Income, pension income, and scheduled withdrawals from 401K and Individual Retirement Account (IRA) funds. Other forms of passive income include annuity income, disability income, income from a rental property, income from a reverse mortgage, and royalties from an intellectual property (e.g., like a published book). What makes the money *passive* is the fact that you've already put in the work for it by saving or contributing in some form. Let's talk a little bit about some different kinds of passive income. What is detailed below is more general in nature. For personalized advice for your specific situation, I strongly advise you to seek advice from a financial planner.

Social Security Income. It's simplest to think of this as a national pension within the United States (Other countries have similar systems). While the funding structure of Social Security is complicated, it follows this basic formula for individuals: each year of work means more social security taxes you pay, which means in turn a higher monthly payout when you begin to draw on benefits. Social Security Income is paid for life, making it a strong foundation for retirement income. There are some complicated rules, such as the fact that you must work at least ten years to qualify. As well, your monthly payout is based on your highest earning 35 years of work. The Social Security Administration always uses the average amount from the highest 35 years, even if you worked fewer than that! Any year below the total of 35 is calculated by adding "zeros" into the equation, meaning your total amount will be less for each year you don't work. Finally, your total is also calculated by the age that you begin to draw on benefits. The younger you are, the less you will get each month. On the other hand, beginning your withdrawal at a younger age means you will get it for *more* months of your life. Withdrawing early can lead to a large percentage of your monthly income being cut, so it is generally a good idea to wait as long as you can. Because life expectancies are ever increasing with the advance of medicine, you'll likely want a higher payout to carry you through. As well, there are payout penalties for earning work income above a certain amount if you receive social security before your designated retirement age. The youngest age you can start to withdraw is 62 years old, and current soon-to-be retirees (Those born after 1960) must wait until 67 years old to receive the full payout. Delaying further, until 70 years old, will even earn you a slight increase (but again, this means fewer overall months withdrawing the funds). As well, the government occasionally increases social security payments by a set percentage point to keep up with inflation, known as the cost of living adjustment (COLA). There are a lot of rules!

For a married couple, both spouses can draw their social securities independently, meaning two sources of income. When one spouse dies, the surviving spouse receives the higher of the two values. In other words: if Person A receives $3,000 per month and Person B receives $1,500 per month, then they make a total of $4,500. If Person A were to pass away, then Person B would receive $3,000 total. If Person B were to pass away, then Person A would receive $3,000 total. This is another reason why it is helpful to delay withdrawing from social security, as it may mean a larger sum for your spouse after you pass away.

Pension Income. A pension is a lifelong retirement payout received from a former employer. Very few industries continue to offer pensions, and those that do are often physically demanding professions. Professions within the United States that still offer pensions include government employees (like postal workers), firefighters, police officers, and members of the U.S. military. Other professions, including those with strong unions, also offer pension plans. In many cases the individual has to opt in for a pension, so make sure you check with your Human Resources department if you believe you are entitled to a pension at retirement. Much like Social Security income, pension payouts are based on your highest salary and total years worked. There is often a minimum total of years you must work to qualify, and you often have to wait for a minimum age before you can start to withdraw.

Investment Income. This includes money you yourself have chosen to save away in anticipation of retirement. The two most common account types designed for retirees include the 401K/403b and the Roth Individual Retirement Account (Roth-IRA). Both accounts involve a wide range of choices for investing your money, such as the stock market or bonds, and both accounts result in a tax penalty if withdrawn before the age of 59 and a half. The 401K (for private industry jobs) and 403b (for non-profit jobs) are what are called "Tax-deferred" accounts, meaning you contribute money that is not taxed at the time of contribution. The 401K/403b money is typically taken from your paycheck before factoring in taxes, and it will not be taxed until you withdraw it. Note, this means that you will have a lower tax bill during the year of contribution, yet you will then be withdrawing "taxable income" in retirement each time you make a withdrawal! The maximum amount you can contribute each year is $22,500 as of 2023. For those aged 50 years and older, the maximum amount has been raised to $30,000 each year due to what is known as "catch-up contributions."

Roth-IRA accounts are unique in that you have already paid the tax on the money when you make a contribution. When you come to withdraw it in retirement, though, you get it tax-free! There is also a lower limit for how much you are allowed to contribute each year, being $6,500 for those below the age of 50 years old and $7,500 for those aged 50 years or older who qualify for the "catch-up contributions" rule. Financial advisors strongly encourage this type of account, as it allows for less taxable income in retirement, meaning they can help their client remain within a lower tax bracket while still withdrawing a comfortable wage. There are also income limits preventing Roth-IRA contributions for high-earning workers, though a "back-door Roth-IRA" contribution can sneak around this limit with no penalty. A personal accountant or financial advisor can help facilitate this kind of maneuver.

While it might feel like too little, too late for some, investing into the above accounts past the age of 50 can still make a strong impact on total retirement funds. Especially since many workers have made it past big expenses in their sixties–a house may be paid off, the kids have graduated from college–this gives them a unique opportunity to stretch hard and devote energy toward maxing out last-minute contributions. With the catch-up rule, a worker can theoretically devote a total of $37,500 to these retirement accounts each year after the age of 50 years old. Even just making these contributions during the last five years before retirement would mean a total of $187,500 saved, not including interest you would earn! That money could definitely come in handy!

Annuity Income. An annuity is a type of investment where a retiree contributes a one-time lump sum of money in exchange for a monthly income amount. You don't get the contribution back, yet the monthly income amount more than pays for it over time. Annuities are a great way to turn the sale of a house or an inheritance into a dependable revenue stream. Each annuity will differ depending on the financial institution offering it, including the amount they will pay for a given contribution, the length of time they will pay, and rules about market fluctuations. But as a general rule, good annuities offer a 5%+ return and pay monthly for the rest of the retiree's life. For example: $200,000 contributed could mean approximately $1,000 per month deposited into your account every month. Instead of just sitting in a checking account, this allows the retiree to turn a large sum of money into a lasting profit. There can be large penalties if you try to take back your contribution money, so make sure you can do without your funds before devoting them here.

Disability Income. An individual receives disability income when a medical condition prevents them from working (as in Social Security Disability Insurance or an independent long-term disability policy) or can be shown to be caused and/or exacerbated by working conditions (as in Service Connection for U.S. Veterans). Disability income is commonly becoming a way that many people supplement their retirement income, though it is risky to rely upon this money source. The reason is that disability income can suddenly disappear without much warning. I have worked with many retirees who became devastated financially when either the term limit for the disability income expired or the official group that determines the status of "disability" for the retiree suddenly reclassifies them. Unless the disability status is guaranteed "For Life," it is important to understand the rules that determine how long this income lasts. For many organizations, disability income is meant to be a short-term support to help the recipient get treatment and either return to work or survive until they can qualify for social security income. While wonderful to have, it is important not to rely on disability income for the long-term but instead shape your budget to be supported by other income sources.

Rental Property. Real estate is a reliable investment that many financial managers recommend due to its track record for stability and for its ability to grow in value at pace with inflation. When millionaires are interviewed, they often list real estate as a commonly used form of investment. Owning a rental property is one form of real estate investment, and they can take many forms: house rental, apartment, storage units, duplex/triplex/quadruplex, and more. There are many ways that a rental property can be a profitable investment for retirees, including rent from tenants, tax breaks/incentives, and increasing property value over time. There are many expenses to consider as a landlord, including upkeep, property tax, and insurance. But for those who are able to receive consistently high rent, it is possible to cover property expenses, emergencies, and some of their own living expenses. And one of the best parts is you can always sell the property and receive back your initial capital investment! This can be an especially fruitful investment for retirees who have skills in home repair or maintenance. For those who don't (like me!), there are property management companies who will help coordinate tenant selection, rent collection, and repairs for a small percentage of the rental income, typically ten percent. With a good property manager, your venture can practically run itself.

Reverse Mortgage. Another form of real estate investment is tapping into the property value of your home, if you are a homeowner. In fact, many retirees are finding that the equity (or monetary value outside of loans) they have in their home residence is one of their largest financial assets. All of those years' worth of mortgage payments will slowly pay off the principal owed on the home, and any increase of home value on the market will also contribute toward the home's equity.

Many retirees are increasingly cashing in on their home equity to supplement their retirement income, and one common way is through a reverse mortgage. To complete this financial maneuver, you must be at least 62 years old and have paid a significant portion (or all) of your mortgage. It works by borrowing a loan from the bank using your home's equity as collateral. You can receive either a lump sum or income payments over time. The downside is you (or your heirs) must pay the loan back once you no longer live in the home, and interest and fees will build up over time. That means your hard-earned equity will be used up over time, and it's very possible that you may end up owing more than your home is worth when you go to sell. This can be a tempting option for retirees who either want to remain in their home or don't want to deal with the trouble of moving. But, as we'll talk about more later on, it typically makes more financial sense to sell one's home, collect the entire value of equity, and then downsize to a cheaper residence.

Royalties. Though unique on a case-by-case basis, it is worth mentioning that some retirees earn passive income from the sales of intellectual property (like a published song) or from allowing a manager to run their business for them. For instance, let's say that an individual is the president of a small yet successful family business and decides to retire. Yet, when he turns around to sell his business, he realizes that he will be hit with a major tax. To get around this, he holds onto ownership of the business, hires a manager to run the operation, and collects an agreed-upon income each month while retaining official ownership. For those who are creative and entrepreneurial, creating educational or entertaining online videos or self-publishing books can also earn passive income over time. Online platforms such as YouT ube.com and Amazon.com have made these processes more accessible and lucrative than ever before.

Active Income. I know it may sound bizarre, but many retirees *choose to continue working in retirement!* One of the main reasons they choose to do this is to help supplement their income, though as we'll speak to more in later chapters, it is not the only reason. In this section we'll discuss paid work and selling assets, both of which involve devoting your energy and time in exchange for money.

Paid Work. Just because you plan on drawing on passive income benefits does not mean you cannot also work for income at the same time. Keep in mind that there is a special rule for those who draw on social security income before their official designated age (currently 67 years old if born after 1960). Any money earned above $21,240 (as of 2023) will result in a financial penalty for that year. The money limit eases in the year leading up to the official designated age such that your financial penalty is lessened. Once you reach full retirement age, there is no limit to the amount of money you are able to earn in retirement from paid work.

One of the obvious purposes of the rule is to discourage people from drawing on social security income before their designated age. In other words, high earners are encouraged to continue working until age 67 if they can to both minimize the penalty and increase their overall social security income payout.

The rule, too, also seems to acknowledge that social security income is often not adequate alone for covering all expenses, and so they allow for supplemental paid work: up to $21,240 per year. Many retirees choose to work on a part-time basis, meaning income continues to come in both from Social Security and work, yet they have more free time as "part-timers" to enjoy themselves.

Selling Assets. While not exactly paid work, there is a lot of effort and stress involved in selling assets. Anyone who readies and sells a house will attest to just how much work is involved! Selling an asset can be a wise decision for three big reasons: 1. You receive money for it; 2. You no longer have to pay upkeep for the asset; and 3. You no longer have to stress or worry about the asset. Common assets that can be sold include a home residence, a business, a work of art or costly antique, and an insurance policy (Yes, you can sell an insurance policy!). The money from the sale can then be used to create a passive source of income that will sustain you throughout your golden years. For example, selling a home can generate a large sum of money, and in turn some or all of that money can be invested into a lifelong annuity.

Again, there are many ways to generate income in retirement. Much of what you choose will be determined by your individual circumstances and tolerance. I want to say again that a financial advisor can be so very helpful for creating a sound financial plan and for avoiding unnecessary taxes. In the future, know you can speak to a financial advisor or an accounting CPA if you find yourself needing some extra support. Think of it as hiring an expert to be on your team! But for now, let's spend some time briefly examining retirement expenses in more detail.

Expenses

We often think that our expenses are set in stone, yet we actually have more control over expenses than one would think. Take a look at the four categories of expenses that you completed for your expense worksheet: Hard Expenses, Soft Expenses, Savings, and Luxury Expenses. Each one can be reduced significantly–yes, even your hard expenses! We become so used to our current circumstances and comfortable with how things are that it is easy to ignore the alternatives. Have you ever heard the expression, "I'm a creature of habit?"

Well, making changes to your circumstances and adjusting your habits can work in your favor to lower expenses. I'm not talking about big changes to your routine, but small and more manageable steps. If we can take many small steps, then they will lead to big differences not just when added together, but also over time.

As an example, consider a pack of cigarettes. The current price, on average, for a pack of cigarettes in the United States is about six dollars. If you smoke one pack per day, then added up over time it will equal $42 each week. Throughout the course of a 30-day month, we're looking at $180 of expense. 365 days at a pack a day equals $2,190! Changing this one habit can save you $2,190 per year. Imagine what you could do with that money: buy roundtrip airline tickets to Europe, remodel your bathroom, or treat yourself to a nice steak dinner twice a month. Even reducing your cigarette use to half of a pack per day means saving $1,095 per year. That is a large chunk of change!

Now, I'm not insisting that you quit smoking (although it is a good idea!). What I am trying to demonstrate is a principle of managing expenses. If we can reduce or even completely eliminate an expense, then it will result in large savings over time. As well, making multiple small steps will combine to help you save even more! Quitting smoking and reducing your time in the shower, for example, will help you save both on your grocery budget and on your water bill. Shop at the discount supermarket and thrift stores instead of high-end businesses for a similar long-term result.

Many people are pleasantly surprised to discover that their expenses naturally decrease organically when entering retirement. For example, working less means spending less on commuting, and many countries offer discounted health insurance once you reach a certain age (such as Medicare in the United States). Overall, as you read through your expenses again, think about ways that each item on your list can be either eliminated or reduced. While some cannot be eliminated completely, most can be reduced in some way. We'll talk about creative ways people have reduced their hard expenses to help demonstrate adaptable thinking.

Reducing Hard Expenses. There are many ways to save when it comes to your "bedrock" monthly expenses. First, we should always think about *downsizing*. Consider moving to a less expensive home or moving to a cheaper area of the country. States like Florida, Texas, Tennessee, and Nevada are especially popular due to their low cost of living and zero-income tax policies. For those who are homeowners, imagine selling a theoretical $200,000 home in your current state and buying a cozy, more manageable condo in Florida for $100,000... thereby pocketing the $100,000 leftover in the process! Downsizing can also come in the form of selling extra vehicles (thereby saving on insurance and upkeep) and eliminating unnecessary subscriptions. Cable TV service is a prime target for downsizing due to the increase in popularity of streaming services. Instead of paying upwards of $200 for a cable TV package, many retirees are buying an Amazon Fire Stick or Roku box and then paying a fraction of the cost of cable for the two or three channels they actually watch. We so often pay way more than we need, due to recurring subscription expenses. As an added bonus, you may find that having fewer expenses will mean fewer things you need to worry about!

Another helpful strategy is to *shop around*. Many services, such as car insurance, phone and Internet providers, and even health insurance supplemental plans are provided by different, competing companies. Due to competition for consumers, some companies will have lower fees than others. The above principle also holds true for the goods you buy at the store, such as grocery items or clothes. Consignment shops can sometimes offer great deals for high-quality clothing or furniture. It takes a little bit of work upfront to find the cheapest deal, yet it will pay dividends in the long run.

Finally, we want to think about ways to *share costs*. Sometimes many hands bear the load better than one person alone. I have to hand it to people for the creative way they've been able to reduce their individual expenses by sharing the costs with others. It's becoming increasingly common for people to take in a roommate or boarder into their homes, thereby saving on rent or mortgage fees. If this sounds like an unsettling prospect, then keep in mind that your new roommate could be a family member or friend! In fact, the amount of intergenerational households is on the rise with families of two and sometimes three generations cohabitating under the same roof. The world seems to be growing ever more expensive, and many young people welcome the opportunity to split expenses with a trusted family member. And, don't think for a second that cohabitation is a one-sided deal because different people can bring different strengths to a household. Maybe Person A makes more money, but Person B enjoys taking care of the kids. Perhaps Person B is good at walking the dogs, while Person A has skills in keeping a budget or providing emotional support. Some friends will share streaming service login information so that all can benefit. For example, if three friends each pay for one subscription, then all can access three streaming channels for the price of one.

Exercise 4: Valued Budgeting

The above are meant to be examples of how to cut down on hard expenses, but know that the principles can be applied to any kind of costs: hard, soft, savings, and luxury expenses. And if it feels like you have to sacrifice or compromise your values by cutting back, then you are not alone. Making major lifestyle changes can generate a lot of hard feelings. Popular opinion suggests that being frugal is a sign of maturity and wisdom, but this is not true for everyone.

Like most things in life, expenses are a tradeoff—when we spend our money on one thing, it means we have less money to spend on other things (be they in the present or the future). Money is a finite resource! And for that reason, creating a budget is actually a helpful exercise for self-discovery because it forces us to identify what is personally important. Take a look at your budget again and ask yourself: *What am I willing to prioritize?* What are the most important items on your budget, the things that you want to spend your hard-earned money on more than anything else? What are the expenses you would be willing to preserve if times grew hard, even if it meant spending less money on other things?

Creating a budget is not just about reducing expenses, but it also is an opportunity to *increase* spending on the things that really matter. If you have all of your basic needs accounted for, then it makes sound sense to enjoy yourself! So as you look at your budget, I want you to circle the three expenses that are the most important to you. Say to yourself: "My life in retirement would not be complete without ____." This is the kind of the expense we are looking for. If you have more than three, then that is fine! If you have fewer than three, then I recommend you to add more. I strongly encourage you to make space in your budget for items of personal meaning and enjoyment, even if it means spending a little less on other things. I once had a patient say to me: "Dr. Penn, I feel like I'm surviving, but I'm not really *living*. Each day feels like eating white rice and drinking plain water." Don't let that be you! You have permission to splurge a little bit, as long as you maintain a comfortable balance—having a budget will allow you to do that. There is something to say for enjoying life while you have the means and ability.

For some, their most important item is their home, such that they will prioritize maintaining and enjoying it. For others, retirement would not be complete without traveling, and so they always manage to store away extra funds each month toward their travel fund. Maybe saving money to spend on gifts for grandchildren is important enough to circle, or maybe your life is lived to the fullest when you can enjoy a night out at your favorite restaurant. There is no wrong answer as long as the item is important to you. One patient I worked with loved horses and always made sure she had enough money to stable and feed her horse. Find what speaks to your heart, and take your time to decide if nothing stands out right away.

When you have circled three or more, I now encourage you to rank them in terms of how important they are to you. Let the number "1" represent the most precious thing, as this is the item in first place, and so on. Not only can this help with prioritizing funds, but actually ranking your important items helps to even better determine what is important for your retirement life. Our goal is to make the most out of your time, after all!

Financial Phineas Revisited

Phineas and his spouse spent a couple of hours calculating both their income and expenses. And while painful and frustrating at first, they felt better informed once they knew how things actually stood financially. Their current expenses outweighed their projected income, and so they determined together which expenses could be cut or reduced. Among other things, they decided to sell one of their vehicles, cancel their cable subscription, and go out to eat once per week instead of four or five times, as they were used to doing. They also determined it would be good to sell their home because, even though they were still paying the mortgage, they would be able to walk away with a sizable amount of equity from the sale of their home. With that money, they decided to buy an inexpensive condo in a cheaper city and put the remainder of their money into investments. Their bills would be cheaper in a smaller residence, and their investments would pay a monthly dividend. To make up for the remainder of their deficit, Phineas's spouse volunteered to get a part-time job, stating: "I actually like to work. It gets me out of the house!" They decided that any extra money would go into their travel fund, which was their top-ranked priority expense/savings goal. If they saved wisely, they figured they could travel to a different state every year until they could cross all fifty off of their bucket list. They were especially looking forward to Hawaii and Alaska.

Check-In #3

We have now gone over the fundamentals of budgeting for retirement. Not an easy task! As before, fill out your responses to the following two questions and be curious to see if your scores have changed over time. On a scale of "0" to "10," you will select which number best describes your current mood with a "0" meaning "Not at all," a "5" meaning "half and half," a "10" meaning "Completely," and including all of the numbers in between.

I feel down and worried when I think about retirement.

I am a _____ out of 10 at this time.

I feel confident in my ability to lead a happy and successful retirement life.

I am a _____ out of 10 at this time.

Summary

The transition into retirement can be challenging, as for most retirees it means adjusting to a new financial situation. Humans are creatures of habit, and we get so used to spending in a certain way after so many years of working. But, as we've discovered, balance can be (and inevitably is) achieved, so never fear! By taking the time to analyze your situation at this point in time, you are now more prepared to achieve that balance. Well done! You deserve a pat on the shoulder or hand for wading through this dense chapter. But I am confident that putting in the work now will pay dividends in the future, in more ways than one.

One last consideration to mention before ending the chapter on financial topics: estate planning. If you intend on leaving an inheritance to your heirs or beneficiaries, you will want to speak to an estate planner in order to protect your assets. I have, sadly, worked with many patients within nursing homes who have seen their life savings dry up in a matter of years or even months due to high fees for care. And there is little that can be done about it at a certain point. I will go into more detail during the next chapter, but for now all you need to know is this: financial assets under your name within the past five years are vulnerable to being seized as sources of payment for high medical care costs. Properties you own, financial investments you have, large purchases, and even financial gifts you make can be linked to you and seized unless given certain legal protections. The rules are complicated and nuanced, so if leaving an inheritance for your loved ones is important to you, then I highly recommend you speak with an estate planner.

GOLDEN RULE 3: HEALTHY LIFE, HAPPY LIFE

It's no secret that health care costs are expensive, especially in the United States. Even more telling, financial managers are increasingly recommending their clients to establish fitness routines, stating: "What is the point of saving for a good retirement life if you don't have the health to enjoy it?" This is just one example of many that planning for retirement involves more than just financial readiness! We'll see how health is tied to not just your physical wellbeing, but also your mental and financial wellness. In fact, we devote a whole chapter to health because it may be the biggest determining factor on how much (or how little) you are able to thrive in this stage of life.

Anyone can agree that it is better to be healthy than not; it is a good idea in theory! Yet, the degree to which we make our physical health a priority can vary from person to person. Some people devote a lot of time and energy to physical wellness, while others do not. Why is this? The first major reason is that being "healthy" or practicing "healthy behaviors" is a tradeoff. When we choose to eat a salad because it is good for us, it means that we choose not to eat a cheeseburger or pizza (or other comfort food). Going for a walk means that we are not in front of the television enjoying a good show, as we cannot be in two places at once. Even going to bed early happens at the expense of enjoying late-night entertainment. To be healthy is an intentional choice, and there is a degree of sacrifice that many health gurus do not acknowledge.

The second main reason that people do not prioritize health and wellness is related to our mindset as a nation. In the United States, we are a people of "fixers." When something is broken, we fix it! And if it ain't broke? You guessed it: we don't fix it! With the best of intentions, we Americans as a whole tend not to address health concerns until they've evolved into a bigger problem (aka, until it's "broke"). And who can blame us, when we spend so much of the work week... Well, working! By the time something is "broke" we go to the hospital looking for a "fix," yet in many cases the damage is done. When a stroke occurs or Diabetes Mellitus Type 2 fully develops, there is no surgery or miracle pill that will get the person back to 100%. In fact, some of the greatest barriers to a happy retirement life are not a lack of funds or a fancy home, but the following:

Obesity.

Diabetes Mellitus Type 2.

Dementia.

Cardiovascular Issues.

Depression.

Chronic Obstructive Pulmonary Disease.

All of the above are preventable, and one focus point of this chapter is talking about each in detail.

Medical doctors are tearing their hair out trying to encourage their patients to engage in behaviors that will prevent these negative health conditions ahead of time. Yet, the old way of thinking is so ingrained that it is an uphill battle. The goal of this chapter is to encourage you to shift your thinking more toward *preventing* life-limiting illnesses. I admit that this is not the most enjoyable topic to read, but I am including it because it is so *very* important for your quality of life in retirement. I have witnessed too many retirees suffer from preventable conditions! This chapter may be difficult to read, and I will do my best to keep it fun. And, the following chapters after this one are much more positive and motivating! Nevertheless, we have to clear this first. To ensure that you have the ability and energy to enjoy your golden years, the work of developing good health habits really needs to start today. And, the steps we need to take are not too hard!

As we'll see, the key is not a crash diet or an expensive fitness program, but fun and simple adjustments to your life. Just as you invest in your financial health, let's also invest in your physical health! You deserve to have a healthy body during your golden years!

The Hard Truth About Health

Health is often viewed as a personal choice. Now, I meet many clients who say, "I'm the one who is smoking or drinking or eating in a certain way–it's not like it's affecting anyone but me. It's *my* health, let me do what I want!"

Yes and no.

It may be true that your body is the only thing affected by your actions in the short-term (although second-hand cigarette smoke is just one example of the negative indirect effects our actions have on others). Yet, in the long-term your choices will have a large impact on not just you, but also your loved ones and even our greater society. The reason is that most medical conditions are treatable now, *though not curable.* Let me explain. Medical science has advanced astronomically in the past few decades, and one result is that previously deadly conditions are not nearly as fatal as they used to be. As a colleague of mine once put it, "Dr. Penn, it's hard to die in this country." Though conditions like heart attacks, strokes, and acute respiratory failure are still deadly, it's much more likely that a victim today will survive the ordeal compared to the low chances our ancestors had in the past. But, after surviving these medical traumas, the patient is usually much more limited in terms of movement, physical strength, mental ability, and capability of caring for themselves. The condition is treatable, but the patient is left with incurable disability.

And now they need to rely on some degree of caregiving from family, friends, and/or trained medical staff.

Sadly, I have seen so many independent clients lose their strength and have no choice but to rely on others to take care of daily tasks. For example, poor diet can lead to the development of Type 2 Diabetes Mellitus, which (among other things) can result in incontinence and even the amputation of feet due to the development of diabetic ulcers. Combine this with obesity, and now the person is bed bound and must rely on someone to help with changing clothes during an incontinence episode. They will also likely need help with bathing, food preparation, and transportation. I'm guessing this is not how you were hoping to spend your retirement, and it certainly is not what your family and friends were hoping for! And, if there is no one around who can help, then the only options are hiring a professional caregiver or entering into full-time nursing home care. Both options are very costly and will quickly dry up your funds; especially nursing home care.

In fact, entering a nursing home can signal the end of financial independence. And, it can happen very quickly and without warning, especially if the individual has done a poor job maintaining their physical health. This will require another long explanation, but bear with me. When an unexpected health decline occurs, a retiree goes to the emergency room, where they are told they must first go to physical rehabilitation before returning home. At the physical rehabilitation facility/full-time nursing home, the retiree typically has about 30 days to meet the therapy goals before insurance stops paying. If the retiree is not able to meet the goal that the physical therapist sets, then the retiree is not able to return home safely. The retiree could technically leave, yet they will be branded with the negative label of "Leaving against medical advice (AMA)" and may be forced to pay for all services rendered. If the retiree must stay beyond thirty days, then the retiree must pay for their stay out of pocket, and the costs are enormous for room, board, and full-time nursing care. In 2021, the national average cost for a private room at a nursing home was approximately $108,000 per year, or $297 per day. That price, unfortunately, is only going up. The retiree is required by law to pay for his or her stay, too, and all assets connected to their name within the previous five years can be identified as sources of payment. This means that the retiree's family must sell all properties, vehicles, and investment accounts connected to the retiree in order to pay for their nursing home stay. Soon the retiree's assets are so depleted that they fall below the poverty level, at which point they can now qualify for Medicaid (which will pay the cost of a nursing home stay). The process of selling off assets to qualify for medicaid is known in the industry as "spending down" the nursing home resident, and it is a very common practice. Remember that brief paragraph about financial trusts in the previous chapter? Well, it's the only way to protect your hard-earned assets from Medicaid and their team who investigates all of your financial activity from the previous five years. Your spouse is entitled to some protection (such as usually being able to keep the house and some discretionary income), yet overall your financial stability has just disappeared in a puff of smoke... And all because of health.

The good news is that life-limiting illnesses are preventable, with very rare exceptions! My goal is to help you to avoid the need for long-term nursing home care for as long as possible. In the next sections, I've narrowed in on some of the most common (and preventable) conditions that result in needing nursing home care. Following this, we'll discuss health behaviors you can start now to help protect your independence. But first, let's check in with Henrietta Health's story from our first chapter.

Example: Henrietta Health

Henrietta had always worked desk jobs: insurance sales, office manager, and human resources representative. While not very physically demanding, she spent much of her workday seated. Plus, the stress could really build up! When the pressure grew severe she would turn to M&M's and Coca-Cola, her favorite snacks. In fact, she was always known around the office as the person who *loved* M&M's. At her recent annual health check-up, her PCP warned her that she was now pre-diabetic and would develop Type-2 Diabetes Mellitus if she did not change her diet and activity level. Henrietta hoped to retire soon, but now she feared that her days relaxing on the beach would be marred by finger pricks for sugar levels and insulin shots.

Henrietta felt lost and confused. The idea of having a life-long condition scared her; she had always been relatively healthy! Sure, she was never finishing any marathons, but she had never been through a health scare like this before. She felt helpless to change things and fearful about what other medical conditions may impact her in the future. Let's examine now some of the most common medical issues facing the elderly. Note: all specific facts related to health disorders featured below is summarized from findings on the National Institutes of Health (NIH) website (NIH.org).

Common Medical Issues

Obesity. Weight can be a sensitive topic, but it is important to talk about. How much we weigh is determined by adding up many things, including the weight of our bones, muscle, retained water, and fat stores. These, in turn, are influenced by genetics and our eating and exercise behaviors. I'm not going to tell you how much you *should* weigh because it's going to be different for everybody! I'll leave that to your primary care doctor. But, there are some helpful trends about weight to understand in terms of health and longevity.

First, everyone has a personal healthy range of weight, including a low number and a high number. If we weigh too little, then we are considered to be underweight; too much, and we are classified as overweight. Both come with their own unique health issues, but in terms of longevity and overall quality of life, it is often more concerning from a medical standpoint to be overweight. It is okay to be classified as overweight, especially if that's what your body gravitates toward naturally! At the same time, the more overweight we are, the greater the odds and the higher the risk of developing other health problems. When we weigh much, much more than our personal range of weight, then we eventually become classified as "obese," and the health issues become even more severe. Physical issues connected with being overweight and obese include:

Difficulty breathing due to increased pressure on the lung wall
Bone and joint pain due to increased strain
Skin breakdown as a result of friction and trapped moisture
Cardiovascular disease due to increased high cholesterol and added strain on the heart
Development of diabetes mellitus
Interference with quality sleep due to constriction of the throat

All of the above can interfere with your ability to get up and engage with the things you enjoy. Imagine you are wearing a backpack all day, and each extra pound on our bodies is like a rock placed inside. Those rocks will make every step heavier and wear down your joints faster. They will make it harder to keep your breath. Since life is a long journey, even removing one rock will make the going easier and pay dividends in the long run!

Further, there are aspects of older age that make obesity particularly problematic. First, for various reasons our metabolism–or the way our body processes energy and naturally loses weight–declines over time. That means we burn fewer calories as we get older, meaning it is much easier to gain more weight in the form of body fat. As well, due to body aches and physical disability, it can be harder to engage in the physical activities that help burn away the fat naturally. In this way, we all become more susceptible to weight gain as we get older, meaning it is all the more important to be intentional about our weight-management behaviors.

Another complication involves taking certain medications as we get older. Some medications we take are called fat-soluble, meaning they are absorbed by body fat from the bloodstream, where they work to do what they need to do. Many drugs, including certain anxiety drugs, pain management drugs, and heart drugs, are fat-soluble. Part of what makes these drugs effective is that they hang out in our fat stores for a long time, releasing slowly. When we have a larger proportion of body fat, these fat-soluble drugs can actually build up too much, eventually leading to an overdose of whatever the drug is! Medical doctors know this, and so they will prescribe lower doses of the drugs that you need in order to prevent a medical emergency. When we are characterized as obese it is much more likely that we will get too little or too much of a drug for a serious medical condition, such as an abnormal heart rhythm. The odds of under-treating a disorder or causing a medical emergency due to overdose increase.

One final concern relates to mobility, and it is a serious one. Our bones and our muscles carry the weights of our bodies–when we carry more weight in the form of body fat, it can lead to significant difficulties with getting around. An older body struggles to maintain muscle mass as effectively as it did when younger, and certain other conditions can weaken our bones, such as osteoporosis. This means that carrying large amounts of weight in the form of body fat can jeopardize our ability to get out of bed in the morning, or walk to the car, or stand in the kitchen to prepare a meal. Especially after a major surgery or recovering from a broken bone, heavy weight can make it difficult to be successful in physical therapy, even if a person is effective at building back their lost muscle mass. I have worked with countless retirees who go to the nursing home after the hospital for physical therapy and are unable to meet their goals well enough to return home. And the reason? The extra body fat they carry means they have to progress more in physical therapy than they otherwise would need to. Many people cannot build back up the strength to lift the weight. Some even are forced to be bed-bound with no chance of discharging home again.

If you find this section to be discouraging, then never fear! Truly, the hope is just to maintain one's weight *well enough* to prevent health issues and continue living life without unnecessary barriers. We'll talk about some simple, minimally intrusive ways to accomplish this. Crash diets–or tricks/meal plans to help you lose an excessive amount of weight in a short time–are both dangerous and are proven to not work in the long run. Anything that causes you to lose more than one pound per week is not healthy and will likely cause you more problems than benefits. If you are worried about your personal amount of body fat, then adjusting your level of activity and calorie intake in *small* ways will actually help the most! We'll talk more about exercise and diet later in this chapter.

Diabetes Mellitus Type 2. Diabetes Mellitus (Otherwise known as just "Diabetes") is a complex medical condition that, when diagnosed, is chronic. This means that it does not ever fully go away. You can take steps to put the condition into remission, yet there will always be the risk that it will come back again. As we'll discuss, the benefits of preventing Diabetes way outweigh the costs.

The mechanism for developing Diabetes is complicated. In short, it is a resistance to insulin at a cellular level and an overall loss of insulin caused by obesity, poor exercise, and increasing age. Insulin is a hormone that helps us to absorb energy into the body, especially energy in the form of sugars–we desperately need it! By developing a resistance to this hormone, our bodies are not as effective at maintaining themselves. Insulin is like motor oil for a car engine or conditioner for hair! Without it, unprocessed sugar will build up in the blood, where over time it can cause serious damage. Long-term effects of untreated Diabetes include:

Frequent Urination
Severe Thirst
Unhealthy Weight Loss
Fatigue
Wounds That Do Not Heal
Heart Disease
Stroke
Neuropathy (Fiery Pain Like Burning Needles)
Blindness
Kidney Failure
Low Blood Flow

Amputations

Some of these symptoms are very serious! Neuropathy feels like burning from a never-ending fire, and kidney failure can lead to toxicity in the bloodstream. Many diabetics have to subject themselves to the surgical removal of their feet and fingers due to poor blood flow and unhealed wounds that become infected and cause cell death. Because high and low levels of sugar can be dangerous for the body, a person with Diabetes must test their blood constantly. Usually this takes the form of pricking one's finger and applying blood to a test censor, though devices now exist that will monitor your sugar and send the results to your smartphone. Diabetics usually test their blood sugar before and after meals, meaning subjection to finger prickings 4-6 times per day. Trust me, it becomes tiresome very quickly! The blood results are used to inform how much supplementary insulin should be administered via injection to help maintain a healthy level of sugars in the blood, meaning a supply of insulin must be kept handy at all times. And for those who don't know, insulin is very expensive and requires refrigeration to keep it fresh and viable. Because the condition requires constant maintenance, results in terrible side-effects, and relies on insulin injections, Diabetes is quickly becoming the main reason people need nursing home care. It is bad news, very common, and worth preventing.

And how do we prevent it? Diet and exercise. Diabetes Mellitus Type 2 is highly likely to develop from a long history of eating sugars and carbohydrates. It's not just candy, soda, and desserts that are the problem, but potato-based foods, white pastas, and foods made from dough (like white bread) are huge contributors. Alcohol, which contains a LOT of sugar, is also a big factor in developing Diabetes. Even condiments like ketchup and salad dressings can contain high levels of Diabetes-causing sugar. I bring these facts up not to shame, but to highlight how much sugar and carbohydrates are present in our culture's food. It's very hard to get away from it! But being intentional about the foods we eat and incorporating light, yet recurring exercise into our daily routines can do a lot for preventing Diabetes. Diet and exercise are even shown to change a current diagnosis of Diabetes into remission, making the management with insulin injections unnecessary. In other words, diet and exercise are the keys, and it's never too late to make a positive change!

Dementia. Thirty, even twenty years ago, medical doctors were terrified of telling a patient when he or she had a positive cancer diagnosis. It wasn't so much because cancer is a terrible disease for the patient or because the patient would become upset; no, the reason that medical doctors were so reluctant to provide this news was because they couldn't do anything about it. Medical doctors, who were supposed to have an answer for any bodily problem, felt helpless against the high lethality of cancer. None of the treatments doctors recommended were very effective, not until the 1990's. Nowadays, doctors do have effective treatments and can screen for and treat cancer. They are not averse to naming the diagnosis because they can do something about it.

Dementia, unfortunately, is the new "cancer." It is the word no one wants to hear come out of a medical provider's mouth, and when it is spoken the advice that goes along with it is usually not very helpful. At this point in time, there is no reversing the diagnosis, nor is there a cure for it except for a very few and rare circumstances. And, the rates of diagnosis are increasing at an astronomical rate–this is because the typical age of onset occurs around 55 years at the earliest and more likely around 65 years old. Because people are living longer, we're seeing more instances of dementia, this late-age disease, than ever before. To make matters worse, our likelihood of developing a dementia increases each year we grow older, such that each decade we live increases the odds of the diagnosis by two times.

Dementia is not well understood, and yet much like cancer, it's likely that we all know someone who has been affected by the disease. "Dementia" is actually an umbrella term for the many subtypes of cognitive (or "brain") disorders, much like "Cancer" is an umbrella term for the lymphoma, melanoma, breast, prostate (and other) types of cancers. The type of dementia a person has is determined by the area of the brain that is affected, the cause of the damage, the age at which the damage occurs, and the way the patient is affected. The two most common subtypes of dementia are dementia due to Alzheimer's disease and vascular dementia (or dementia due to a stroke). Alzheimer's disease involves damage to the part of the brain called the hippocampus, and it is most known for the effect of memory loss. An individual with Alzheimer's disease struggles to create new memories, and so may not remember what they had for breakfast or what you told them five minutes ago. Vascular dementia, on the other hand, can be caused by damage to one of many different areas of the brain by either one large stroke or a series of many smaller strokes termed "small vessel disease." A stroke occurs when something either blocks a blood flow channel in the brain (such as a blood clot) or bursts a blood flow channel (such as in a case of high blood pressure). People with vascular dementia typically struggle with completing complex tasks, have difficulties with movement/drawing, and show signs of mood alteration. Alzheimer's disease gets progressively worse over time, and vascular dementia may improve and stabilize with time; yet, suffering from a stroke makes it much more likely that you will have another stroke in the future, thereby leading to a decline over time. Other forms of dementia come from Parkinson's disease, traumatic brain injury, Huntington's disease, excessive alcohol abuse, damage to the frontal or temporal lobes of the brain, and more. To make matters more complicated, medical examiners are determining that most people now (and probably in the past, too) actually have multiple forms of dementia all at once, called "mixed dementia." As is clear, researchers are working hard to understand the dementias and still have much more work to do!

In testament to how important the brain is, people with dementia are soon unable to live independently. With enough time, a person with dementia will develop severe memory impairment, struggle with language, act out emotionally, feel impaired with movement (and become a risk of falling frequently), and lack the means of taking care of themselves, no matter what subtype or types of dementia they have. Because of this, having a moderate-to-severe dementia is the leading cause of needing full-time nursing care, usually at a nursing home. While there are some medications to help slow down the rate of memory loss for a short while and reduce unpleasant behaviors, there is no known cure yet for dementia.

Even though there is no cure, there is strong research evidence suggesting that we can delay or even prevent dementia through healthy behaviors. Risk factors for developing dementia include: poor exercise, poor diet, poor sleep, tobacco use, depression, and lack of engaging/enjoyable activities. So, we can help protect ourselves by creating reasonable habits around exercise, nutrition, sleep, and doing things we enjoy. If you've been at all on the fence about making any healthy changes, let this be the wind behind your sails! We want to prevent dementia at all costs.

Cardiovascular Problems. When we talk about the cardiovascular system, we mean all of the parts of your body involved with transporting blood to where it needs to go. Your heart works 24/7 to pump nutrient- and oxygen-rich blood through veins and arteries and to your brain and other life-sustaining organs. The cardiovascular system is vital; if it were to stop working, we wouldn't last for very long. This is one of the reasons why heart disease is currently the leading cause of death in the United States, beating out both cancer and COVID-19. So we'll spend some brief time discussing it here.

While there are some genetic factors that contribute to the development of heart disease, a large portion of it has to do with (you guessed it, if you've been following the trend of these sections!) diet and exercise. The heart is a very resilient organ and adjusts its rhythm very well to the needs of the body. That being said, anything that causes it to work harder for a prolonged period of time can lead to fatal consequences. Your veins are like a series of hoses throughout your body, and your heart pumps blood steadily through these hoses. Veins filled with cholesterol and fats from the unhealthy foods we eat or the gunky plaque found in cigarettes will constrict the hose, meaning the heart has to work harder to push the blood where it needs to go. This is called "high blood pressure," and here is where we have the problem because a build-up of pressure has to go somewhere. Sometimes the arteries will burst or become damaged, which is the equivalent to puncturing a hole in a thick hose. When this happens in the brain, we call it a stroke. Another possibility is that the heart will continue pumping, yet parts of the circuit become so blocked up with bad stuff that areas of the body are unable to receive life-sustaining blood. Known as peripheral artery disease, the most likely places that blood flow will fail to reach are the arms and legs, often requiring major surgery or even amputation. Another possibility is that the pressure will push on the heart, resulting in damage or even heart failure (a.k.a., a heart attack). Even if minor, heart failure can significantly impair a person for the rest of their life, limiting the person's ability to perform everyday tasks and lowering overall energy level. Some people even lose the ability to walk independently.

To prevent heart disease, we therefore need to limit the artery-blocking substances we allow into our bodies and find a way to clear out the existing substances from our veins. Simply put: eat a diet low in fats and unhealthy cholesterols, refrain from smoking, and make sure to exercise. Moderate exercise is one of the most effective ways of preventing heart disease because it lowers cholesterol and fats, and it trains your heart to be able to better pump blood. Think of exercising as a power washer designed to clear out your veins and help them work at their best! So by decreasing the harmful blocking agents going in and cleaning out the ones already there (even just a little bit!), we can make a big difference.

Depression. While not a physical disorder per se, it is worth mentioning because of the sinister way it impacts physical health. Depression is a terrible disease of the mind, and its symptoms include low/sad mood, lack of pleasure in daily activities, significant weight loss or gain, sleeping too much or too little, feeling and acting restless, low energy, feeling worthless or no good, trouble concentrating or coming to a decision, and thinking often about dying/not wanting to live anymore. Of note, if you believe that you may be experiencing these symptoms, especially the first two and the last one, then I strongly encourage you to speak with a licensed mental health provider. *PsychologyToday.com* is a great resource allowing you to find therapists who will accept your health insurance. For those not wanting to live anymore, the national suicide and crisis hotline is a great, free service designed to connect you with someone who can help you feel better, no matter the time of day. Even those not feeling suicidal but are nevertheless in great emotional distress are encouraged to call and will receive help. The volunteers are really kind and understanding (I would know, I used to work at one of their local offices!). Just dial "988" to get connected with a volunteer.

There is an assumption out there that depression is a normal part of aging. Well, this assumption has conclusively been proven false! In fact, research shows that quality of life actually improves as we grow older, due to a natural process of negative emotions numbing over time. Most surveyed adults say that they are able to enjoy life despite illnesses or physical concerns. So if you do find yourself feeling blue, it is *understandable* because life circumstances can be very difficult! But it is not *a given* aspect of growing older and can be treated with the right help. Talking to a counselor or asking your medical doctor about a low-dose antidepressant can be a great place to start and is often sufficient for turning things around.

There are a lot of important reasons to treat depression, too. I refer to depression as a "sinister" disease because it undermines the very steps needed to treat it. A common example of a depressed person is someone who avoids company, doesn't eat, sleeps poorly, neglects personal hygiene, doesn't want to move, and experiences self-pity. These symptoms are the complete opposite of what a person needs to do to overcome the disease! Beating depression means we need to spend time with others, eat nutritional meals, get good quality sleep, take care of ourselves, exercise, and view our traits and actions as positive. Left untreated, depression can literally cause the body to break down. Muscles weaken, skin develops infections, and we are more likely to collapse from weakness. Many people also express depression in the form of anger, making it more difficult to retain and cultivate relationships. There is a common saying picking up in popularity regarding depression: "If you don't want to go to therapy for yourself, then go for the sake of your family and friends." Very likely the depression is having a negative impact on the people close to you. Depressed individuals are also more prone to alcoholism or seeking other substances in an attempt to temporarily improve mood or cope with stress. Finally, and perhaps the most important issue with depression, it increases your risk of developing dementia. Studies are increasingly finding that having prolonged, untreated depression can actually be a strong predictor of developing dementia in the future. The reason for this is unknown (as much about dementia is at this time), but scientists speculate it has to do with inactivity and poor sleep. Regardless of the reason, the link is there. Attending mental health therapy or taking medication can seem like a high cost to some, but not if it means preventing the tragic condition of dementia.

I know that the above is negative and doom-and-gloom talk. To some degree it is meant to be, if only to stress the importance of caring for your body. I wish I could say that these negative health conditions represent rare experiences, but they are quickly becoming the norm. At the very least, ask yourself this: Would I rather experience all of the fun and excitement of the next two decades with a sound mind and body? Or would I choose instead increased pain, shortness of breath, and poor memory? Let's focus on making the former option your reality. And it is an option! No matter what stage in life or physical condition, there are things you can do to improve your wellness and increase your longevity. In 2011, the first man over the age of one hundred years old completed a full marathon. Nicknamed the "Turbaned Tornado," Fauja Singh began training as a runner in his seventies and has inspired many others aged seventy and older to also complete marathons. Hidekichi Miyazaki and Donald Pellman were also noted sprinters who set world records after the age of one hundred years old, and Miyazaki specifically did not take up running until he was in his nineties. It goes to show that it is never too late to change your health for the better! We'll talk about some ways to do that in the section below.

Positive Health Behaviors

The following sections are meant to be small steps anyone can take to improve their longevity and quality of life. I am not proposing a massive overhaul to your day, just little things to be added that, in the long run, will guarantee a big return on investment. Even just making an adjustment in one area can help you to feel better, weather changes, and save you money. How? Integrating positive health changes into your life can help prevent serious disease, maintain your favorite activities for longer, and save you money on medical bills.

Primary Care Appointment. Meeting with your primary care provider at least once per year is extremely important. Not only is a yearly wellness exam fully covered by most insurance plans, but a medical doctor can help you to detect any changes that occur in your body. As we grow older, organs just don't work like they used to. Kidneys and livers filter less effectively, glands secrete less effectively, and maintenance medications change according to age. For women menopause can signal a major adjustment in what the body does, and the same goes for men who experience prostate issues. By seeing you once a year, a primary care provider worth their salt can pick up on changes in bloodwork, weight, and cognitive (or mental reasoning) ability. Using this knowledge, they can then prescribe treatment to help prevent many serious health conditions, including diabetes, stroke, heart attack, lung disease, and more.

One helpful strategy I recommend to all people of all ages is to keep a running list of questions you have for your medical doctor. I can't tell you how many times I've left my primary care provider's office, merged onto the highway, and then remembered too late that *one important question* I wanted to ask her. Keep a list! And if your doctor explains a concept in a way that you don't understand, I strongly encourage you to ask for clarification. Phrases like, "Can you tell me more about

X? I've never heard of it before," or "I didn't catch that, could you explain it in a different way?" are always welcome with a good provider. Keep in mind that a medical explanation or instruction directly affects you and your body–you're the one who has to live with it, and your doctor is being paid to explain it to you accurately. Don't be afraid to ask questions, follow-up questions, clarifications, and even more questions! And, if you find that your primary care provider is not helpful in the way that you need, feel free to change to another one. It is a common practice, and medical doctors are used to it. You deserve a provider who is a good fit for you.

So make a list now, either on a notecard or in a reminder application in your smartphone, of questions you want to ask your doctor during your next visit. You may have one already, and if so, excellent job. If not, this is a great time to start! Further, I would add the following question to your list, and in the next section we'll explore why: "Given my physical ability, what is a good level of exercise I should try to achieve each week?"

Exercise. Moving your body contributes in so many ways to your health! Exercise in any form not only helps to reduce body fat, but it also helps to maintain muscles, keep joints flexible and limber, improve energy level, reduce the risk and symptoms of diabetes, foster quality sleep at night, and reduce the risk of developing dementia (to name just a few benefits!). Not only does it help with physical wellness, but many people find exercise to be fun! There's actually a chemical reason for this: when we move, the body releases endorphins. Endorphins are a "feel-good" hormone that help to reduce the perception of pain and reduce stress; they're pretty great, and all natural! Our brain releases them to counteract the normal wear-and-tear that comes along with movement, but the added bonus is they help reduce *overall* pain levels and inflammation. That means we can use exercise as a form of pain management, and many chronic pain psychologists actually use this principle to help their clients reduce their pain levels. Ever notice when you have a lot of stress on your mind that going for a walk helps organize your thoughts and feel better about whatever is going on? It's thanks, in part, to endorphins!

The U.S. Department of Human Services currently recommends spending 150 minutes walking each week, though any walking is better than none. Considering there are 10,080 minutes in a week, this doesn't seem like a big commitment! To meet the goal of 150 minutes, many people will spend 30 minutes per day, five days per week walking while others try to get 20 minutes each day. Consider walking around your neighborhood or see if there is a local park nearby. Some individuals choose a day to walk through the mall, especially when the weather is poor. Routine walking can be a great way to structure your schedule each week, and pairing it with other enjoyable things can make it even better. You could walk regularly with friends or family, while others may choose to listen to music or pair it with bird-watching. I personally enjoy buying a cup of specialty black coffee and listening to an audiobook while I walk.

If walking isn't your cup of tea (or cup of coffee!), other forms of exercise are also very fun and beneficial. Many people find great enjoyment in doing Tai Chi with a group, which is a light form of slow martial arts movements that benefits thinking and balance. Other people find chair yoga to be very enjoyable, where they follow along with an instructor performing stretching exercises from the comfort of a seated position. One patient I worked with was unable to walk, yet he exercised everyday by lifting soup cans above his head. I am convinced that a form of exercise exists out there for every interest and ability level. For this reason, it's always helpful to check in with your primary care doctor before beginning an exercise routine; not just to generate new ideas, but also to see if you can perform the activity safely. Exercise is not helpful if it causes us to fall or over-strains our system.

I very often hear people say as they are beginning a new exercise routine: "I'm not going to exercise today because I don't feel like it" or "I'm too tired to exercise." These statements are valid and true, as they speak to how we as humans typically view *rewards*. We very often gravitate toward actions that we find rewarding *right now*. To illustrate, consider which of the following two choices sounds more enjoyable: relaxing, or getting tired and sweaty? Now let me ask you, how would you feel an hour from now if you relaxed versus relieving stress through exercise? Looking back over the day, which choice would bring you the greater sense of pride and satisfaction? More likely than not, we all would feel more satisfied, positive, and just plain *good* if we spent some time exercising. This is the downside to making choices based on how we feel: our feelings are better at telling us what we want *right now*. For activities that are rewarding in the long-term (such as exercise), we have to think about how we'll feel in the future. This is one of the keys for long-term motivation, and we can use it for any instance in which we need to accomplish something tedious, draining, or hard.

Instead of: "I'm not going to exercise today because I don't feel like it," try to say: "If I exercise today, then I'll feel better."

Instead of: "I'm too tired to exercise," try to say: "If I exercise, I'll have more energy."

Beginning anything new is hard at first and takes commitment. It can be easier, though, if we schedule special time for the activity. This leads us to our chapter's exercise: scheduling exercise!

Exercise 5: Scheduling Physical Exercise

This is one of the shortest exercises, yet it is still equally important. Very simply, I encourage you to write down when your time to exercise will be during the week. If you have a planner or calendar, then this is a great place to do it. If not, then a plain sheet of paper will do–just make sure to place it somewhere important and visible.

It doesn't matter what the exercise is–walking, swimming, chair yoga, pickleball, or all of the above! What matters is that by writing it down, you are one step closer to committing to this very important practice for improving your life and maintaining your good health. Try to schedule at least 150 minutes total throughout the week to receive the best benefit. Maybe you feel more motivated in the mornings, or maybe you're looking for a way to structure your time between lunch and dinner. Your scheduled time can look as simple as this example:

Sunday: Rest

Monday: Walk 8:00 to 8:30am

Tuesday: Walk 8:00 to 8:30am

Wednesday: Walk 8:00 to 8:30am

Thursday: Walk 8:00 to 8:30am

Friday: Walk 8:00 to 8:30am

Saturday: Rest

Feel free to revise in the future if a different time works better for you! But for now, try to get some times down on paper.

Diet. If you think about it, we consume all of the energy, nutrients, and compounds we need for our bodies to run effectively in the form of food. Carbohydrates give us immediate energy, proteins provide upkeep for muscles, fiber helps the digestive system to run smoothly, and fats protect sensitive organs and facilitate the absorption of vitamins and minerals. Much like gasoline and oil for a car, food is the fuel for our bodies; but unlike a car, we can't easily replace a part or trade in our bodies for a new model! To make it last and keep it running smooth, feed your body the right fuel.

There are a lot of get-thin-quick diets out there that receive a lot of media attention, but these are not what most medical doctors recommend. It's not a difference of opinion or a preference for one style over another: "Crash" diets just don't work, and there are two main reasons. First, your body gravitates toward a specific weight unique to you, and if you lose weight too quickly then your body won't have time to adjust. Like a rubber band, your weight will rise again soon after ending the diet, until you find yourself right back to your original weight. The second reason is that severe calorie restrictions and eliminating important foods completely can take a dangerous toll on the body. Crash diets actually push the body into a state of malnutrition, resulting in a loss of muscle and bone mass as the body attempts to draw nutrition and fuel from energy reserves. It can also strain the heart, sometimes even resulting in a heart attack or other forms of permanent damage. Be wary of diet programs promising weight loss of more than 1-2 pounds per week.

General consensus among medical and dietary professionals at the time of writing this book is that the Mediterranean diet is highly effective for weight management and longevity. It's actually the diet of a town with the largest concentration of centenarians, or people who live to be 100 years old, in the world (It's called *Acciarolli* in Southern Italy)! The Mediterranean diet is based on the foods commonly eaten by towns bordering the Mediterranean Sea in Southern Europe, specifically Greece and Southern Italy. The cuisine mostly centers around lean meats like chicken and fish, as well as plenty of vegetables, beans, nuts, and complex grains. Most of the cooking and preparation is done in olive oil. This diet encourages people to avoid red meats, alcohol, heavily processed or preserved foods, butter, and refined carbohydrates like sugar or white bread. The diet is so effective because it contains a balance of food types that is not too different from what most people are used to eating. For example, a typical dinner might be grilled chicken with a side salad and wild rice. You still get your proteins, fats, and carbohydrates, but the ingredients are leaner and fresher. For this reason, more people are able to stick with the diet until eating the foods becomes an established habit. And the diet is effective: people who adhere to a Mediterranean diet have been shown to experience lower rates of obesity, diabetes, stroke, heart disease, and even dementia.

Dietary changes are not required to be sudden and drastic. Just changing one meal per day or even one side dish per day toward a Mediterranean diet can help you experience health benefits. Just keep finding ways to add the foods in over time. Even replacing soda pop with water or unsweet tea can lead to significant changes over time. For instance, if a can of soda pop has 200 calories, and you drink one can per day, then that is an extra 6,000 calories you are consuming each month. That is the equivalent to gaining *2-3 pounds* each month. Imagine if you just eliminated that soda!

See if there are small changes you can make, and check in on how you feel after. My guess is your body will feel more energized and clean, and that's what I want for you. You deserve to treat yourself to the healthiest food made on this earth, especially since it's not too expensive! Much like with exercise, the self-talk that we use can really help with new dietary habit-building: think about how you will feel in the future (even later in the day!) after eating a balanced Mediterranean meal. "If I eat this, then I will feel better and more energized. My heart, waistline, brain, and digestive system will thank me!" And, make sure to pat yourself on the shoulder or hand after each healthy meal because you deserve someone to tell you that you did a job well done.

If you are interested in learning more about the Mediterranean diet, then I encourage you to look up recipes on the Internet or ask your primary care provider for more information. Your doctor may even refer you to a dietician for assistance, and insurance will often pay for the visit.

Sleep. Most people can agree that sleep is important, and most know that getting seven to eight hours is recommended each night. Studies throughout history show that sleep deprivation can result in a mental breakdown or even death (I am grateful I was never a part of those studies!). You may notice after a poor night's sleep that your mood suffers, your body aches, and it is difficult to think clearly. It's hard to have a good day when we don't get our beauty rest!

Sleep serves many functions for the body. As we move throughout the day, our muscles and tendons experience micro-tears and wear down. Sleep is actually when the body repairs this wear-and-tear, which explains why we physically feel so poor after a bad night's sleep. The body needs a chance to heal! As well, the brain releases a special fluid during sleep that washes out all of the gunk and refuse that builds up throughout the day. Without this process, the built up particulates can interfere with optimal brain functioning, leaving us feeling groggy and slow. There is even strong evidence to suggest that Alzheimer's disease and other forms of dementia are caused, at least in part, by the buildup of too much "brain gunk." In this way, sleep is for the body what a tune-up is for your car. The difference is, we need a tune-up every day!

Most people enjoy sleep, but for some it is difficult to prioritize it over other things they would rather do. Staying up late often involves entertaining late-night TV shows or is a chance to be alone without anyone else around. Be that as it may, we should not sacrifice sleep unless it is an emergency. Sleep deprivation works on a two-week average, meaning if you get a poor night's sleep on day one, you will feel it for the next thirteen days unless you can make up for the lost sleep. For those who nap, try not to sleep for more than twenty minutes during the day, or else you may interfere with your ability to fall asleep at night.

To help with falling asleep, try to limit caffeine and alcohol in the evenings and avoid bright screens, which will trick your brain into thinking it is still daylight outside. Do calming activities as you get ready for bed, like reading a book or listening to soft music. Bedtime is not the time to solve problems or worry about the next day–save that for another time! And because we are such creatures of habit, we begin to create negative mental associations with the bed if we toss and turn for more than twenty minutes without falling asleep. We want to associate rest and sleep with the bed, not frustration and stress! So, if you find yourself unable to sleep for more than twenty minutes, break the association by getting up and doing a calming activity until you feel sleepy. Then, try again. I know it sounds simplistic, but this practice can break insomnia. If you find that you continually have trouble falling asleep, staying asleep, or getting the full seven to eight hours, consider working with a sleep therapist who uses a treatment protocol called "Cognitive Behavioral Therapy for Insomnia." Such a guide can help retrain your habits and get you back to sleeping well. Your body and brain will thank you!

On a final note, there is an important distinction between *quality* and *quantity* of sleep. An individual may sleep eight or even ten hours and wake up feeling groggy and sore, meaning the quality was actually poor. While it is true that humans tend to wake up more frequently as we get older, it's still normal to get good quality sleep. If, on the other hand, you find that you typically get a good *quantity* of sleep but consistently feel fatigued and slowed in thinking, then it may be a sign of a sleep disorder. The most common sleep disorder medical practitioners see is one called Obstructive Sleep Apnea, or "OSA," in which the airways in a person's throat close periodically during sleep. The most common signs of sleep apnea are fatigue during the day and snoring at night. Each time the airways close, the body literally suffocates and causes the individual to temporarily wake up. These wake-ups can happen dozens or even hundreds of times *each night*, meaning the throat constrictions prevent the individual from entering deep, restorative sleep. It almost sounds like torture, and the results can be just as bad if left untreated. Side effects can include fatigue, poor mood, a faster onset of dementia, and even hallucinations. That is how important quality sleep is, and how important it is to seek treatment for this condition. Your medical provider may suggest wearing a CPAP mask during sleep to prevent these brief episodes of suffocation, and the bad news is most people find them to be uncomfortable. The good news is that there are many different models of masks to try and that they become more comfortable over time.

Cigarettes, Alcohol, and Drugs. I cannot conclude a chapter on health behaviors without mentioning cigarettes, alcohol, and other drugs. Most people who use these substances understand the side effects and are willing to accept the consequences. I understand, and I can respect that! I will take a few paragraphs, though, to share how these substances affect the body differently as we age. The body handles things in different ways when we are older compared to when our bodies are young and operating at peak performance. After reading the following, you can make an informed decision.

Cigarettes. We know that chronic use of cigarettes and nicotine products can increase your risk for cardiovascular disease, including majorly debilitating diseases like heart attack, stroke, and limb amputation due to poor circulation. We also know that smoking increases our risk of developing different cancers and will tax our lungs. What many people may not realize is that smoking can cause permanent damage to the lungs when we are older. Our bodies are less flexible and resilient, less able to bounce back and repair when cells die. For our lungs, this means that their capacity to hold and process oxygen declines over time when we smoke, and for many this leads to a permanent condition called Chronic Obstructive Pulmonary Disease (COPD). Individuals with COPD are unable to get enough oxygen when they breathe and become reliant on oxygen tanks, which contain higher concentrations of oxygen. This means carrying an oxygen tank wherever they go and buying special equipment for their homes. Some living arrangements are unable to support supplemental oxygen equipment, meaning the individual must move to somewhere that can support it. As well, using nicotine products can also prevent an individual from receiving important surgeries. Surgeons use a complicated decision-making process to determine who will or will not be a successful surgery candidate, taking into account factors such as age, weight, and existing medical conditions. Because nicotine slows and interferes with the natural healing process, many surgeons will refuse to operate on a patient if the patient uses nicotine products. Speak to your primary care doctor if you are interested in quitting smoking or using other nicotine products!

Alcohol. The body responds differently to alcohol as we age. Apart from increasing our risk of developing diabetes due to the high concentration of sugar in alcohol, the ability of our liver and kidneys to process alcohol out of the bloodstream declines over time. For this reason, the amount of alcohol we used to be able to drink when we were younger will now cause much more damage in older age. The brain is also more sensitive, and exposure to alcohol can cause an even greater degree of drunkenness. Drinking also increases the risk of developing dementia, too. And, it can interfere with or even nullify the effects of medications we take for other life-limiting illnesses—medications we didn't need to take when we were younger. For this reason, we should only indulge with alcohol on rare occasions, if at all.

Other Drugs. Other forms of drugs, such as amphetamines (like cocaine or crystal meth), heroin, and marijuana, are risky to take at any age. But, like the sections above, our bodies are more sensitive to the negative effects of drugs as we grow older, and such drugs can combine with our other medications in deadly ways. Heart attack, respiratory failure, stroke, and seizures all grow more likely in an older body. Marijuana in particular has been gaining acceptance in the greater culture, claiming to be non-addictive. Well, the research evidence is suggesting that it is, in fact, addictive for some (much as practically anything can become addictive!). Emergency department visits have been on the rise for older adults in particular related to marijuana-related situations. Marijuana use can increase the risk of poor balance and falls, strain the lungs, and result in paranoia and/or deadly delirium. The issue with marijuana is that many strains today are more powerful than what was available in the past, and medical researchers are still struggling to fully understand how it affects the body or interacts with other medications. If you want to use marijuana, such as for pain management, make sure to speak with your primary care provider to discuss dosing and frequency of use. In all things, safety first!

Summary

In short, following this golden rule is not too complicated. A few simple yet highly effective adjustments can make a huge impact on your life in retirement. Eat a balanced, Mediterranean diet; build walks or other forms of light exercise into your day; get seven to eight hours of sleep each night; avoid drugs, including alcohol and nicotine; and meet annually with your primary care provider. If these seem like common sense, then you are correct! But to know that these behaviors, practiced regularly, are *the most effective way* to prevent and reduce the effects of debilitating conditions like dementia, heart attack, diabetes mellitus, and COPD is worth emphasizing. I will risk sounding redundant if it drives the point home and helps people to live longer and more fulfilling lives. And, as an added bonus, these behaviors will help you to feel better, more accomplished, and self-confident. All of the money in the world can't buy that; remember, practicing a good habit costs you absolutely nothing but time. And in retirement you will have much more control over how you spend your time, which is a truly valuable resource. Please consider investing this valuable resource into your physical and mental wellness. You deserve it!

I also want to emphasize that if you have a chronic health condition, then that is no reason to despair. The health behaviors we've covered above will help provide relief to the symptoms you experience, prevent further decline, and reduce the risk of developing other conditions. We all have difficulties, and there is a strong genetic factor in the development of a disease or condition. And, what's in the past is in the past! Choosing a more healthy lifestyle gives each of us the best chance moving forward, from this day on. It is never too late to start!

Pat yourself on the hand or shoulder because you've made it through a dense chapter! Not always the most enjoyable of topics, but the golden rule of health is too important to ignore and meet unprepared. Now, though, you have some skills and a game plan for how to proceed in this arena. Well done! We'll wrap up this chapter by checking in once more with Henrietta Health to see how she managed to adapt to her new health concerns.

Henrietta Health, Revisited

Henrietta interpreted the news from her primary care appointment as a wake-up call. Instead of despairing, she asked her doctor follow-up questions about how to prevent any serious issues and decided on a game plan. She began to go for light walks in the evenings and replace one meal each day with a recipe from her new Mediterranean diet cookbook. Soon she found recipes that she really liked and would cook for herself each day, but she just couldn't bring herself to enjoy walking. She tried listening to podcasts and changing the location, but it just wasn't her thing. She didn't give up! When passing by the local YMCA on one of her walks, she noticed they had an indoor swimming pool. She remembered how much she enjoyed swimming and signed up. Soon she was swimming laps everyday with a relaxed, easy rhythm. Over time the exercise helped her to sleep better, and her sugar levels remained at the pre-diabetic level for over a year. Then, at a follow-up appointment, she received the good news that she no longer qualified for prediabetes status and would no longer have to concern herself with blood sugar levels! She was enjoying her new routine, felt energized, and was looking forward to building more self-care time into her upcoming retirement. She even still enjoyed the occasional fun-size bag of M&M's, but things felt much more balanced now.

Check-In #4

We now have a general understanding of how to maintain and even improve our physical health during retirement. With this information in mind, let's check in once more on your feelings and sense of confidence about retirement. On a scale of "0" to "10," you will select which number best describes your current mood with a "0" meaning "Not at all," a "5" meaning "half and half," and a "10" meaning "Completely."

I feel down and worried when I think about retirement.

I am a _____ out of 10 at this time.

I feel confident in my ability to lead a happy and successful retirement life.

I am a _____ out of 10 at this time.

GOLDEN RULE 4: GET YOUR HOME IN ORDER

B eachfront property. Condos. The old family homestead. A series of RV campgrounds. Cruise ships. Assisted living facilities with 24-hour care and onsite chefs. Ex-pat communities in foreign countries. Retirees more than ever are breaking the mold by living in a wide variety of places. While some are able to reside in the same home for decades, this is becoming increasingly less common and for a variety of reasons. Some move to a new living situation for factors outside of their control, while others pick up and migrate somewhere new for the opportunities it presents. There is a lot of variation in people's decisions, and so the focus of this golden rule will be to help you be clear about housing in retirement.

Despite changing trends, people tend not to imagine themselves moving in the near future. Why might this be? Recall Residential Reginald from Chapter 1–let's revisit his story real quick:

Example: Residential Reginald

Reginald lived and worked in the same area of the country where he was born and raised. Life was good–there were friends always at hand, and he knew the area well. As time went on, though, his children moved away to other cities for school and work, and his friends seemed to slowly disappear, for one reason or another. Plus, things around town were getting so expensive! And, it didn't help that he was starting to have trouble with the stairs in his home. His old stomping grounds just didn't feel the same. Soon he found himself self-isolating at home and feeling miserable. For the first time, he thought about moving to a new area. But, the thought of packing up all of his stuff and moving to a new place was overwhelming. He didn't know what to do, but he knew that something had to change.

Though it seems like Reginald has many good reasons to move, it's not quite that easy. We become attached and comfortable with our homes, not to mention the fact that moving is a lot of work! Whatever doesn't get packed needs to be sold, donated, or disposed of. And, moving fees always end up being more expensive than anticipated. For these reasons people only tend to engage in such an undertaking in response to either (1) necessity: such as a new medical disability or accident to the home; or (2) a fantastic opportunity: something big or exciting enough to outweigh the costs of moving.

Such positive or negative events and the accompanying stress we have to deal with are often hard to see coming. The objective of this golden rule is to try to take some of the uncertainty out of housing adjustments in retirement. By knowing what other retirees have had to deal with and opportunities they took advantage of, you can better know what to consider and why regarding your own evolving situation. The following sections are things to consider. Some may apply to you, others may not, and a few you may never have thought to look into. As you read, consider not just your current situation but also try to imagine ten, twenty, even thirty years from now. How might your needs be different? Have you always dreamed of living somewhere special, and would you be disappointed if you never took the leap? These are the questions that have no definite right answer, but going through the sections below can help you to feel more prepared.

The Trouble With Stairs

Stairs, step-ups, inclines—these are the greatest yet most sinister foe of any retiree with goals of remaining in a long-term residence and should be considered. This is because we often take for granted the fact that we will always be able to use the stairs, much as we've done our entire lives. And I'm not just referring to stairs in a staircase; porch steps, garage steps, and even the step up onto the curb in front of your home can all become serious obstacles. Over time, but especially after unforeseen accidents, we begin to lose the ability to lift our feet, move them forward, and place them safely and securely onto the ground, multiple times in a row. If you think about it, it is a complex series of "steps" to take a step!

Because of this, steps are probably the top reason (or at least top two) that prevents a person from returning home after a hospital stay. If you are unable to make it into your house safely, then you are not safe to return home in the eyes of the hospital medical team and you will need to go to a physical rehab facility. All because of a step! The medical team is being overly cautious, yes, but the risk of having a fall is actually serious business. Even accounting for the possibility that someone else will be present in the home to respond immediately to a fall, it still means a high likelihood of breaking a major bone (like a hip or shoulder) or hitting your head against the wall, floor, or furniture. Consider stepping over the rim of your bathtub onto slick porcelain—it can be an accident waiting to happen for many. In many cases a fall can be fatal. Steps make it much more likely that you will fall if you become unsteady on your feet, plain and simple.

Falling aside, there is also the consideration of strain on your body. Walking up and down a flight of stairs can grow very tiresome. I remember in my house growing up, the washing machine and dryer were down in the basement. Boy, let me tell you, lugging baskets of clothes up and down those stairs was not fun for my back! Think to yourself looking around your current home and any future homes you consider: "Am I going to want to deal with these steps for the rest of my life?" Consider the same if you have a sunken den or loose carpets/rugs. Anything can be a tripping hazard in the wrong place. Do any rooms have crooked or slanting floors? If you live above the ground floor of an apartment building, imagine what you would do if the elevator broke down and needed repairs. Would you be able to leave for doctor appointments or groceries? Would you be able to get back?

There are some things you can do to take care of these concerns ahead of time. There are services (some of which are free) that will install ramps up to your front or back door, allowing you to have at least one reliable entrance/exit into the building. There is a booming industry of plumbers and contractors who will replace your bathtub with a step-in tub or walk-in shower. Handrails can be installed along walls, special equipment can be purchased, living rooms can be converted into downstairs bedrooms. Basically the only deal breaker I would look out for when considering a lodging is whether or not it has a ground floor entrance to your private space. Keep these things in mind when deciding about where you'll live, and it will save you a lot of trouble in the long run. And, if you can, address environmental warning signs before they become an issue!

The People Around You

For many, home is where the heart is. Who we choose to spend our time with has a huge impact on our mood and overall satisfaction with life. If your relationships are your strongest value in life, then you may want to strategize on a way to live close to them. This may mean moving to a new place to be closer to friends and family, or it may mean prioritizing ways to stay in your current area of the country. Even living close to an airport offering regular direct flights to your loved ones is an important option to consider and for many may be the best one. It's good to have the flexibility of an airport nearby. The reason is family members and friends can have an unfortunate tendency to move away for perfectly reasonable new opportunities or changes in circumstances... Meaning if you moved to be close to them, then you now may be left living in an unfamiliar city or town with no close kin.

When considering living somewhere, try to spend a significant amount of time in the area. Travel there, spend the night, experience it during different times of year. Florida, for instance, can be lovely in the early parts of the year, yet it is a muggy, choking swamp come summer (Take it from someone who grew up there!). When getting a feel for a place, try to get a sense of the culture around you. Do you get a good feeling from the people? Do you like their pace of life, the popular activities they do, the way they view the world? How about the food? Do they have any tips for what it's like to live there? Vacation in the area as a tourist, but keep an eye out on what it's like to be one of the locals. In short, you'll want to look for people you "gel" with, who feel like they're part of your "tribe." If you do feel at home with the local groove, then you can be more confident that the area is a good choice–no matter how the plans of your friends and family may change in the future.

As has briefly been touched upon in the chapter on financial readiness, cohabitating with family members can be a win-win situation, especially when it comes to cutting costs and sharing labor for all parties involved. There are many ways to make this work, including co-purchasing a duplex, placing a tiny home next to a larger house, or converting a single home into separated areas. In each potential situation, make sure to be very clear about boundaries–establish how costs and home equity are divided, which areas of the house are private for whom, and how household decisions should be made. Keeping open communication is key for keeping things civil and preventing misunderstandings or resentment.

Cost of Living

Of course, cost of living plays a major factor in deciding where to live. Since we are so mentally focused on the price tag, many people don't think about the reasoning behind this. The typical trend seen nowadays is for established families to retire and move away from higher cost of living areas to areas that are more affordable. While this does create a nice financial cushion, it in turn can result in a loss of benefit. There is a reason that certain areas have a high cost of living!

Typically cities are more expensive than rural areas, but with that expense comes access to better public transportation, better hospitals, more diversity of restaurants, and more entertainment. Certain states are more expensive than others because of the desirability of weather or access to warm beaches. These factors may not be so important at an earlier stage of retirement, but they can grow in importance as our functioning changes. For example, we may not always be able to drive ourselves to medical appointments. If specialty medical care is needed, it may not be within close proximity to certain regions of a given state. One factor many rural citizens are struggling with is a lack of an established courier service to drive them to and from medical appointments–a private service that is much more common in cities. Most city buses even come equipped with lifts for people in wheelchairs. Another common concern is the lack of available medical workers in rural regions, both at the hospital level and at the assisted-living and nursing home levels. Because they require specialty training and can often be paid more in areas with a greater population density, nurses and nursing aides are becoming harder to find in small towns. And it is the patients in these medical facilities that have to cope with the staff shortage. This is certainly not the fault of rural areas, and in fact they need much more financial support than what they're getting. I have been inspired by examples of rural community members coming together to support those in need through church or community-run programs. And, most people I talk to highlight the closeness of nature and the slow, easy-going pace of life in the country as worthwhile benefits. There are pros and cons to all areas of the country.

I realize that I may sound like a hypocrite, as earlier in the book I spoke of the strategy of selling one's home to buy a cheaper residence. This is still an important strategy to consider, yet I want to also stress that it is a tradeoff. For many, it is worth the high cost of remaining in an expensive area. For others, it's not! Many would agree that an ideal combination of factors would be low cost of living and a large amount of benefit: the proverbial "More bang for your buck" scenario. Many states will try to paint themselves in just such a light to encourage people to move there. Know that this benefits the states and may or may not actually benefit the people moving there–it depends. As my grandfather used to say, "Never trust a free lunch." There is always a catch, and always fine print. So let's take a very brief glimpse at some of the most popular states where retirees are moving to at the time of this book's writing. According to AARP (The American Association of Retired Persons), the five states with the greatest influx of retirees in

2022 were Florida, North Carolina, Michigan, Arizona, and Georgia; and the most common reason people cited for moving was to find a lower cost of living.

Please keep in mind as you read the following that I am neither a tax expert nor a real estate aficionado! I merely follow trends and do a bit of researching to find why people are moving. If you are considering a move, always consult with at least two real estate agents in your desired area, letting them know your needs and expectations.

States With The Greatest Influx of Retirees

Florida. Florida has a lot to offer for retirees, including lower cost of living, warm weather, access to beaches, and no state income tax. This means that Florida residents only pay Federal and not state income tax when they earn income... including withdrawals from taxable retirement fund accounts. There is also a high concentration of retirees in Florida, creating indirect benefits of both more people to meet in the same stage of life and a booming healthcare industry catered to older persons.

As a native Floridian, the "Sunshine State" will always have a place in my heart, but trust me when I say there are some costs to living full-time in paradise. Financially, Florida has some slightly above-average property tax costs and very high homeowners insurance fees. Florida knows that it has desirable real estate, and seasonal hurricanes mean that most insurance companies will only accept the risk of coverage if they charge high rates. Due to the heat, utilities costs are often very high as well. Beyond financial concerns, hurricanes can be a deadly nuisance, especially if one is living in a home that is not storm-proofed. As well, areas of Florida are experiencing unprecedented heatwaves, contributing to major health emergencies and even death. The wildlife is also unpleasant to contend with at times, including swarms of mosquitoes, palmetto bugs (a.k.a. Large cockroaches), and fire ants hiding in the grass. Alligator and shark attacks are actually rare occurrences, though the encounters are hyped up by news outlets due to the shock factor (though I do remember having lessons about "gator safety training" in grade school!). Finally, Florida will feel differently at different times of the year as the tourist season ebbs and flows. While the "snow birds" bother some, for others it is a welcome time of excitement–especially for the snowbirds themselves!

North Carolina. The general draw for North Carolina is a combination of lower cost of living and access to natural beauty. In North Carolina you get both mountains and beaches at a relatively affordable price. North Carolina also allows a state tax exemption of $35,000 of retirement income per year, no social security tax, and no estate tax. The income tax rate is also currently below 5%. Combined with the fact that it is centrally located on the East Coast, North Carolina can be the perfect destination for one's golden years. On a personal note, my grandfather retired to Asheville, North Carolina and loved the pine trees, winding mountain roads, and tranquility of the green spaces available. He also received excellent healthcare!

There are some downsides to North Carolina as an option for residence, including the fact that its residents have to deal with the occasional hurricane. While not as often an issue as, say, Florida, the fact that hurricanes are only occasional nuisances mean that many homes are not built with withstanding hurricanes in mind. And those winding roads? Definitely not fun to drive during a winter snowstorm! Another thing to consider is that North Carolina is vast with many different flavors depending on where you live. As with all states, there are some towns in North Carolina that have great transportation and healthcare, while others have more of an off-the-beaten-path kind of feel. There are some cities that report very high crime rates. As has been emphasized before, take a vacation in the area you are considering to get a feel for what it would be like to live there. It worked for my grandfather, but it may not be everyone's cup of tea.

Michigan. My in-laws and wife are from Michigan, and to be completely transparent I was surprised at first to see that Michigan was a popular spot for retirees! But after researching more, I am happy to say that I am eating my words and can completely understand the appeal. Michigan offers so much for retirees, especially for those who want to stay within the midwest. For starters, there is no social security tax and lower than average income tax rates. As well, property values are exceptionally low, and considering the fact that most cities are within driving distance of Great Lake beaches, many find the prices to be a steal. The median home price in Michigan is around $150,000, meaning many homes sell for below this amount. The cost of living is low, and there is a friendly small-town feel along with more urban experiences in areas like Detroit and Ann Arbor. Of all of the states listed here, Michigan may be the most affordable. And it has perhaps more golf courses than any other state, if that's what you're into.

That being said, there are some downsides to living year-round by the Great Lakes. Perhaps the biggest challenge to living in Michigan, according to my in-laws and many others, is the long winter season. Due to the "Lake Effect," snowstorms coming off of the lake can bring freezing temperatures and large amounts of precipitation. And the winter season can drag on for a long, long time. As a native Floridian, you can understand my initial hesitancy to accept Michigan as a retirement destination! On top of this, the winter precipitation leads to poor road conditions and limited to no public transportation in most areas. Having access to a car is almost certainly a necessity. Furthermore, the low property costs come along with high property taxes. So if you can find a cheaper home then it is not so bad, but if you are looking for a more expensive house–say, near the beach–then your property tax burden will likely be steep.

Arizona. Arizona can be an appealing destination for many retirees due to the weather alone, which favors those looking for a climate with dry heat. The property and income taxes are also affordable compared to other states, and they do not tax on social security (noticing a trend in what makes a state desirable?). The fact that there are many retirees moving to Arizona also means that there are growing communities of retirees with readily available clubs and activities to become involved with. Arizona appears to be particularly popular with Californians and people from other surrounding states looking for a more affordable spot to stake their claim. I have a great cousin who actually prefers Arizona to Florida because it is far less muggy and humid.

That being said, Arizona in many ways is the victim of its own popularity. Word on the street is that housing and rental prices are skyrocketing due to the fact that so many people have been moving there lately. And though it has a decent healthcare system, it does not appear to stand out against the national average. This can be a problem down the road for some retirees, especially considering the high heat can lead to risk of heat stroke in the summers. As well, Arizona apparently reports very poor air quality compared to most other states due to air pollution. As with most things in life, there are always two sides to every coin (or three, or four, etc.).

Georgia. Due to its close proximity in the southeast, Georgia shares many of the same benefits as Florida in terms of weather. But, it is certainly not the less popular brother to the sunshine state and in fact stands on its own in terms of appeal for retirees. It offers a low tax burden on retirees, including no social security tax and a tax exemption of $65,000 for retirement income for those over the age of 65 years. Georgia boasts pleasant weather with mild winters and summer temperatures that don't push quite as high as Florida. There is also significantly less risk exposure to hurricanes. On top of that, home prices are generally affordable, property taxes are low, and the overall cost of living is below the national average. This means a lot when considering it's possible to reach Florida, Alabama, Tennessee, South Carolina, and North Carolina all within a reasonable day's drive. And speaking of driving, Georgia does an excellent job maintaining its roads and highway systems, though individual public transportation will vary by area.

The most consistent downside I've been able to find is that Georgia ranks low in terms of entertainment. Most survey bodies agree that Georgia overall has little to do! I know it seems like I have family everywhere from this list, and it's true that I have an aunt who lived for many years in Georgia! I can say from my experiences visiting her that Georgia is peaceful, quaint, and relaxed; but, it is not very exciting, at least from one young person's perspective. One exception is Atlanta, which boasts many restaurants and diverse subcommunities. Another exception is Savannah, which is quite charming and antebellum in feel. Georgia also appears to rank middling in terms of healthcare. But if the slow and easy lifestyle is appealing, while still having the option to travel to other states (especially since Atlanta airport connects to practically everywhere), then Georgia may be the hidden gem you have been looking for.

Other Factors. It's worth noting that people decide to move for many diverse reasons, and following the COVID-19 pandemic people have increasingly chosen to move due to political orientation. Conservative families have flocked to states like Texas and Florida, though it's worth noting that a fair amount of liberal families have as well. What's going on here? Well, cost of living appears to be the biggest driving force for people moving, and it turns out that there are both conservative *and* liberal areas in both states. All the more reason to vacation or take an extended stay in a new area before moving! Others find that a given location can be *good enough* if it gives them easy access to what's really important to them. For example, proximity to a reliable airport may make a cheaper area more desirable. Crime is also something to be mindful of anywhere you live, and at any time of life.

Ex-Pats/Traveling

An interesting trend gaining popularity in the last few decades is for people to retire and move to a foreign country. This is undoubtedly a side effect of globalization, and it's not just an option for people with dual citizenship or ties to other countries (though these things certainly help!). In fact, the main motivator in becoming an "ex-pat" (or "Ex-patriot") appears to be cost of living. Many retirees find that their social security checks go much further in certain foreign countries than if they stayed within the United States. Other factors that retirees find favorable include high quality/low-cost healthcare, ideal climate, and ease of acquiring a visa/citizenship. According to *International Living*, the top ten countries that Americans are choosing for their retirement destination include (in order of popularity): Portugal, Mexico, Panama, Ecuador, Costa Rica, Spain, Greece, France, Italy, and Thailand. Since these are popular destinations, one inherent benefit is the fact that there will be available ex-pat communities already in place for support and developing friendships. Another benefit includes access to travel opportunities from your base country. For example, ex-pats in Portugal can more easily sightsee around Europe, and Thailand offers ease of travel for areas in East Asia and the Pacific. For those with a lifelong case of having the "Travel Bug," this can be a very exciting option to pursue.

Keep in mind, though, that establishing citizenship can be a lengthy and at times costly process. Some countries require a hefty financial investment in property or commercial enterprise in exchange for a visa that will last the five years required to establish residency. Otherwise, each country will have its own rules about how long an individual can remain within its borders under a given visa, meaning many ex-pats must plan regular trips abroad to get around these rules (which is not always a bad thing!). Each country also is a self-contained culture onto itself, meaning both big and small differences in how society runs. And, it's sometimes the smaller differences that are the most surprising, like differences in the timeline for processing official documents or proper rules for conducting oneself in public. Many ex-pats are initially confused or reluctant to seek help in a foreign country when something goes awry, and so knowing where the nearest USA embassy is will be a huge priority.

One last important point to consider is the possibility of entering the end-of-life stage abroad. Especially in a country in which the native tongue is your second language, it can be scary and isolating to need nursing home care. I have worked with many nursing home residents within the United States who do not speak English, and they have a much harder time making their needs known. Ex-pats navigate around this problem by maintaining dual citizenship, yet it can be much harder at times to return to the USA from abroad when we suffer from a newly broken hip, develop a crippling dementia, or experience a sudden loss of funds. As always, do your research and travel first in the country you are considering. That way, you can anticipate future challenges.

For those who love traveling yet value the sense of security that comes with having a home on American soil, consider living near an international airport or shipping port for a major cruise line. Cruises appeal to many retirees, as they take care of lodging, dining, and itinerary all under a predictable price. Cruise ships even have full-time medical staff on call 24 hours per day, including an ICU and options for medivac to onshore hospitals in dire situations. Though costly, these services are available to help provide peace of mind to passengers. Some retirees have been known to rent a cheap apartment or condo and use the money they save to fill up their yearly calendars with cruises all over the world.

Exercise 6: Values for Residence

With so many different factors that influence where to live, it can be difficult to settle on which things are the most important to you. The following is a list of some of the values that influence this important decision. This exercise asks you to take a look at this list and identify the three most important things for you. In other words, which things are your "deal-breakers" regarding where you live? If such a value were not a part of your life, would you still be happy living there? And if you aren't fulfilling your value, is there something you can do to change that? You can identify more than three, and you can add values that are missing–but try to come up with at least three. Once you do, write them on a separate sheet of paper and order them in terms of importance to you. This can take time to think out, and you may find that your list of values is similar to the values you've identified for previous exercises. Regardless, identifying what is important to you can help clarify this overall process.

Values for Residence

Family, Friends, Travel, Country Life, Hobbies, Healthcare, Variety/Adventure, Politics, Transportation, My Community, Cost of Living, Faith Group, City Life, Staying Put, Independence, Low Maintenance, Stability, Scenery, Weather, Familiarity.

Needing Extra Care

This is never a fun topic, though it is an important discussion to have with friends, family, and yourself. If we live long enough, it will become necessary to arrange for extra help. For some that will mean paying for help to come into your home to take care of chores and minor medical needs. For others, having full-time support available will be necessary to maintain independence, and so an assisted living facility (ALF) will be a good option. Finally, for those who need full-time medical care, finding a nursing home may be the only option. It is common to progress gradually through the steps of increasing dependence: from living independently, to living independently with in-home help, to living in an assisted living facility, and finally to living within a nursing home. Some enterprising companies offer arrangements for all of the above, meaning the resident will not have to move when the next level of care is needed, and they can continue to receive services from the same parent company who knows them well. We'll cover each level of added help below, with the pros and cons of each. For those who value planning ahead, it's a good idea to familiarize yourself with the resources available around where you live. If it became necessary to receive extra help, where would you want to go? And how much does it cost?

In-Home Help. As we grow older, it becomes harder to keep up with tasks like cleaning, cooking, lawn-care, and doing the laundry. Imagine all of the movements involved with these tasks: lifting, bending, scrubbing, carrying, standing, reaching, twisting, pushing, and all for an extended period of time! Sometimes trying to do these tasks can result in a muscle strain or even a long-term injury. Thankfully, there is a thriving in-home caregiving industry with both established national companies and independent solo workers ready to perform all of these tasks. Select services will also aid in bathing and providing care for incontinence. There are also elevated levels of this service for minor healthcare concerns, including post-surgery wound care, blood oxygen level monitoring, and diabetes maintenance. For this kind of service, skilled nurses trained for in-home care will come periodically to perform these functions.

It is hard to say what will be covered under insurance, as each insurance plan is different. Typically medical in-home care is covered under most insurance plans, though it is often limited to a certain duration of time (whatever the insurance company deems adequate for the need). Certain home health companies will also only provide medical and custodial services under those insurance plans that will pay well. At the time of this writing, patients are finding it incredibly difficult to arrange for in-home services that will accept Medicaid insurance, as Medicaid typically does not reimburse well. There is also a national deficit in persons working as in-home caregivers, meaning the ones who *are* working do so for the higher-pay companies. This is certainly something to consider when shopping around for insurance plans! For those who choose to pay out of pocket, the price can be steep–the national average clocks in around $5,000 per month, though this varies greatly based on the services needed, geographical location, and frequency of visits. For those who can get by well on their own and need only occasional help, consider enlisting a cleaning service that will stop by once per month. Some people voice discomfort with having strangers work within their home, yet it can be worth the price and discomfort if remaining in your home is valuable to you.

Assisted Living Facilities. Assisted Living Facilities (ALF's) are communities of independent and semi-independent persons who live within an apartment-like building or collection of buildings and receive services from the providing company. ALF's provided cooking, cleaning, transportation, and activities services on site, leading many retirees to liken them to stationary cruise ships or live-in day clubs. ALF's also employ low level medical staff for emergencies and minor health maintenance needs, such as help with administering medications. This level of service is the sweet spot for retirees who are still able to move about independently yet do not want to deal with the hassle of daily chores. Those who are concerned about medical emergencies or living alone also find ALF's to be a great fit, as the staff provide regular monitoring and are knowledgeable about nearby emergency services. And, retirees have a built-in social network available, as meals are usually served in a central dining area and the activities department organizes regular games/socials. The apartments are private, and residents are free to come and go as they please, running errands or visiting with family. This is an excellent option to consider for maintaining one's independence, and it is a good idea to shop around your area to see what is available for the future.

Besides the downside of moving out of one's home and living more closely to others, the biggest drawback to living in an ALF is the price tag. This service is not cheap, though it is significantly less costly than nursing home care. The national average runs somewhere near $4,500 to $5,000 per month at the time of this writing, which for most is significantly more than their monthly expenses. Though, when you consider all that is covered by the price, it can be a very appealing deal: housing, food, cooking, cleaning, transportation to appointments, social activities, and safety monitoring are all included. As well, maintenance costs are covered by the ALF company, meaning any frozen pipes, malfunctioning air conditioning units, and leaky roofs are all someone else's problem, not yours. Another downside is space, as ALF apartments are often efficiency units with significantly less area for your belongings than most homes. Moving into an ALF usually means downsizing by either selling furniture or acquiring a storage unit. You also would run the risk of living near a noisy (or nosy!) neighbor. Further, ALF's have a criteria screen you must complete to see if you have the capability of living at the level of independence needed for an ALF. If your degree of functioning has too many barriers to living independently or your ongoing medical needs are too extensive for the basic medical support available, then the facility will recommend nursing home placement. This also applies to current ALF residents, meaning there may come a point when the ALF can no longer support a person's needs and a move to a higher level of care will be required. Some facilities have both ALF and nursing home care combined so that an ALF resident can transition to the nursing home area when the time comes, though this is not always the case. As such, an ALF may not be a permanent home for some.

One side note: many long-term care companies will offer different payment options, either monthly payments or a large, one-time payment. Companies know that retirees often have large sums of investment monies or great amounts of home equity to draw from. As such, they will often offer to accept a large sum payment–almost all of your money–in exchange for a guaranteed spot for life within their community. In other words, you will not be turned away or forced to find alternative lodgings if you run out of funds. Such an option needs to be considered very carefully, and it is generally a good idea to consult with your family and/or trusted financial advisors (if applicable) before accepting. For those long-term care companies that provide multiple levels of care, such that you could move from their ALF to their nursing home unit and even then to their dementia/memory care unit, this can provide a much needed sense of security and predictability for your future care. For those that don't offer a graded series like this, *buyer beware*. As you may realize, life changes along with our functioning! It's very possible that you will need different degrees of care over time, and agreeing to pay a large sum of money for a "guaranteed spot" at an ALF does not take this into account. In other words, your spot will only remain "guaranteed" as long as they can continue to meet your medical needs. If those needs change–and they likely will–then they are required by law to send you to somewhere that can meet those needs. And such a place may not be bound by the financial agreement you signed! As such, the facility can legally keep your large sum payment and send you elsewhere. If you are considering a "spot for life" kind of deal, then make sure to read the fine print and ask many hypothetical questions. "What happens to the agreement if the facility is bought by another company?" "What happens if I develop dementia?" "What kind of lodgings will I have with this agreement–will I have to share a room?" "Can I choose which doctors I see, or do I have to meet with the facility doctors?" "Are there any reasons the agreement will no longer be able to work, and what happens then?" Obviously choosing to reside in an ALF is a big decision. Make sure to ask plenty of questions and seek guidance from a legal advisor/lawyer if you find the introductory paperwork to be confusing.

Nursing Homes. A nursing home is a place where you can reside and receive healthcare. They come in all kinds of shapes and sizes: some are small, and some are incredibly large. They are typically run by a parent organization that runs multiple facilities. Some companies are deemed "for profit," meaning they are run as a competitive business. Other, less common, companies are deemed "non-profit," meaning they are typically sponsored by a charity organization of some kind. Non-profit facilities usually have more staff available at any given time to help the patients and often do not accept insurance (in other words, you must pay full-price, out of pocket for your stay). For-profit facilities do accept insurance and are more likely to have availability to receive new patients. It is not uncommon for people to wait months or even a year or longer for a spot to open up in a desired non-profit facility! That being said, there are really good for-profit facilities, and really bad non-profit ones. Both types provide access to all needed types of medical care (e.g., physical therapy, vision, audiology, dentistry, internal medicine, etc.) and most have both "long-term" and "short-term" plans. Short-term care is limited to a certain amount of time designated by your insurance company to recover from your ailment, most of the time lasting up to a couple of months. Long-term care covers the time after short-term is over, meaning the patient did not recover enough to return home or has a chronic condition that prevents them from going home.

Long-term care is typically not covered in full by supplemental insurance plans, like Medicare. It happens all too frequently that a patient goes to the hospital and is discharged to a nursing home to recover with short-term care, only to become a long-term care patient. There are social workers on staff who work with patients and families to help get people back home, such as by ordering supportive equipment the patient may need at home. But, if there are issues with the home (like stairs!) or the functioning of the patient, then by law the nursing home advises against discharge. You can see how easy it can be to get "stuck" in a nursing home, especially if your functioning is impaired.

When the words "Nursing Home" are uttered, many people experience an immediate, negative reaction. I hear too often: "That's the place people go to die;" and I believe it is this association between nursing homes and death that creates such a negative reaction. There is the (false) belief that nursing homes kill people, or at the very least hasten people to die faster. Maybe you've witnessed a bad experience with a family member in a nursing home or saw nursing home care a long time ago, when newer and better standards were not yet in place. I believe it is because of this negative reputation that I see clients fight tooth and nail to not enter nursing home care, even if it means going contrary to medical advice. The fortunate fact is that most nursing homes are gentle and pleasant places to reside. The problem is that a few bad nursing homes give the rest a bad name, and there are many reasons why nursing home care can be a good option! Specifically, you will want to consider nursing home care when you develop medical conditions requiring ongoing treatment management and clinical observation by medical personnel. The most common conditions include COPD, dementia, cardiovascular disorders, severe type 2 diabetes, becoming bedridden, chronic kidney disease, and more. Other reasons include not being able to care for oneself and lacking the means to make up for this deficit. These are reasons that an ALF would not be able to support your needs, and at this point a nursing home is an excellent option. The following are positive aspects of a good nursing home that I believe should be considered:

1. It is prepared to care for life-limiting and debilitating illnesses. Nursing homes are staffed by licensed nurses and medical doctors, providing care 24/7. If you suffer from congestive heart failure and need constant monitoring, then a nursing home can be a Godsend. In fact, part of the reason people say "it's the place people go to die" is because the patients typically have life-threatening illnesses/conditions. In other words, it's not the nursing home itself that leads to death but the *medical reasons* that require nursing home care. In research we refer to this as a "confounding variable," meaning the medical reasons actually explain better the cause-and-effect relationship between nursing homes and rates of dying. At times it is easier to blame the nursing home for the loss of a loved one than it is to confront the terrible course of a disease or condition. Having COPD or syncope or dementia or loss of mobility is incredibly unfair–nursing homes are there to

help make coping with these conditions more bearable.

2. It is designed for comfort. By law, nursing homes are required to provide for any patient's comfort and safety while under their care. For this reason rooms, bedding, and clothing are all kept clean, and an Activities Department is in place to provide opportunities for enjoyment. I have worked with many nursing home residents who have lived in the facility for over a decade and feel very much at home there. If you or a loved one find themselves in a very *uncomfortable* facility, then I strongly suggest you seek out another, more reputable one.

3. It can help a family to stay closer. People tend to be at their happiest when their social lives are simple and predictable. There are exceptions, but people work and live well together when they have clear roles. Your spouse is your spouse, your parent is your parent, and no matter what your child says, your child will always be your child. Losing functioning to the point that you need help with taking a shower or changing your briefs after an accident can start to change those very clearly defined roles. Suddenly your spouse is not just your best friend and romantic partner, but now they are also your caretaker: cleaning you, lifting you up out of your chair, counting out your medications, etc. This blurring of the roles can put a lot of strain on your relationships! Going to a nursing home can help prevent this strain: now a nurses' aide can take care of all of the extra needs you have, and you can just be mom or dad, husband or wife to your loved ones.

4. Our culture is changing. Many people reading this have been

caregivers for their family members. It is a noble profession, and it was the most common practice twenty-plus years ago. You may have served as the caregiver for your parents or even spouse, allowing them to stay longer in their home and postpone nursing home care. They may not even have needed to go into a nursing home at all! Sadly, this is rarely possible nowadays based on the people I've interviewed and worked with directly. The main cause for this is economic: it is becoming too expensive to take time away from work and be a caregiver. Most middle-aged and young couples–those who would traditionally serve as caregivers for their aging parents–require both partners to work in order to make ends meet. To be a caregiver means giving up a much-needed paycheck in a world that is growing ever more tight for the middle and lower class. Some families are able to come together to create a mutually beneficial arrangement, yet it is quickly becoming the exception and not the rule. Nursing homes are there to provide the needed care.

5. It is often not forever. In contrast to the perception that nursing homes are "a place you go to die," I have worked with many individuals who were able to discharge home after years of living in a nursing home, either because they worked hard to meet their physical therapy goals or they acquired a new living situation that could meet their needs. If the patient approaches the situation with the right attitude, then staying in a nursing home can be temporary and even helpful for living independently. Patients build up their strength through physical therapy, learn to use new equipment, and acquire new coping skills. Though not everyone can meet the

necessary levels of functioning, it's those who give up that certainly fail.

6. It can be a secure form of housing. For those who meet the medical need, Medicaid in the United States will cover whatever you cannot pay toward a nursing home room. It will mean sharing a room with a roommate, being forced to follow certain rules/restrictions, and diverting any forms of income to the facility to help pay for your stay. In exchange, you will have a place to sleep, three meals a day with snacks, medical care, medications, and access to facility-sponsored activities. Though often the last choice people would make, living permanently in a nursing home can be a smart move if you have little to no savings and struggle to support yourself financially. In 2017, six out of every ten residents within nursing homes were using Medicaid to pay for their room (according to the Kaiser Family Foundation), and it is likely that the ratio is even larger today.

So, while not the first or preferred choice, residing in a nursing home is certainly not the worst living situation. By the time a nursing home is recommended, there usually is not much choice left in the matter—the only comparable arrangement would be 24/7 in-home nursing care, which costs more money than most people have. Oftentimes when we do not have a fair choice, the only thing we do retain control over is our attitude. You can give it a chance, or you can resist tooth-and-nail. From my personal observations, the people who keep an open mind and try to stay optimistic often adjust well and even thrive in nursing homes. Those who fight against their situation, on the other hand, often make their medical conditions even worse through overstraining, resisting treatment, or losing strength due to giving up.

If a family must make the difficult decision to enroll a loved one into a nursing home (or even an ALF), there are some things that can help. First, keep in mind that any kind of adjustment is hard (for instance, retiring!), and it may take months for a person to adjust to a new place. Be patient, and try to stay optimistic. People will get used to most anything with time. Second, ongoing family involvement is incredibly helpful. Having regular visits to look forward to or going on family outings will create a sense of structure for the week and bring variety and joy. Third, taking time to meet the staff and check in regularly will help ensure your loved one continues to receive proper care. Get to know the aides, nurses, social worker, nurse manager, and even the facility director if possible. Seeing you regularly will help engender goodwill and create accountability. It's much less tempting to overlook duties or do a rushed job on a treatment knowing that a family member might come by and notice.

If you do notice something is amiss and staff do not address the concern, call and make a report to the facility's ombudsman, who is an unbiased government-appointed representative whose job it is to address issues in nursing homes. If that fails to resolve the issue, calling and making a report to your state's Office of the Inspector General (OIG) will land the nursing facility in serious trouble. As such, this course of action should only be taken in extreme circumstances; but, do know that it is available for you or your loved one.

Summary

Overall, many factors play a role in deciding where you will live in retirement: preference, cost of living, health, social support, and more. It is not an easy decision to make, and it is one that will need to be revisited multiple times as your situation changes. Knowing which options are available and under what circumstances they should be considered can help you be more prepared. Ask your friends in the area or even your primary care doctor if they could tell you more about ALF's and/or nursing facilities nearby. And don't forget about your personal values, which we discussed in chapter 1–these, too, will play a role in where you want to live and how.

And, remember Residential Reginald? Let's take a look and see how he resolved his dilemma about where to live:

Reginald found that he just wasn't happy anymore staying in his hometown. So, he explored many different options and settled on moving to the town where his daughter lives. He downsized his belongings and bought a much cheaper condo, which helped bolster up his savings. Now he spends his time babysitting his grandchildren and exploring new things in his new town. On top of it all, he only lives a few hours away from his old stomping grounds, meaning he can drive back for a visit anytime. And, though it won't be needed for (hopefully!) many years to come, he has done some light research on good ALF's and nursing homes in the area... Just in case. Life isn't the same, but he's glad that he made the move.

Check-In #5

Even if you plan on staying in your current residence, hopefully this chapter has helped you to consider other options for housing as well as back-up plans. Let's do another check-in, remembering to be curious as to whether any numbers are changing for better or worse. If you find yourself feeling better and more confident, then great! If not, that is okay, too–we'll talk more later as to why this might be. For now, fill in the ratings as to how you feel in this current moment. On a scale of "0" to "10," you will select which number best describes your current mood with a "0" meaning "Not at all," a "5" meaning "half and half," and a "10" meaning "Completely."

I feel down and worried when I think about retirement.

I am a _____ out of 10 at this time.

I feel confident in my ability to lead a happy and successful retirement life.

I am a _____ out of 10 at this time.

Golden Rule 5: Do Something Meaningful With Your Time

C ongratulations! You have come to the most *fun* golden rule! Give yourself a pat on the shoulder or on the hand as a symbolic way of rewarding yourself for making it this far. Up to this point we have covered the nitty-gritty of finances, health, and housing. But now we get to explore how you plan to use your time! There are so many different ways to enjoy the freedom of your time that it can be a bit intimidating. In fact, it's highly recommended that you develop at least a loose plan to help guide what you want to do. Otherwise, it's very easy to drift along, each mundane day blending into the next. Relevant to this, let's take a look again at the predicament of our friend, Free-Time Felecia:

Example: Free-Time Felecia

Felecia was a self-proclaimed workaholic. She thrived in the office, putting in extra hours and strategizing about her next big project or work task. She shaped most of her identity and self-worth around her job, taking immense pride in the praise she received and the money she brought home... So it was an immense shock when she was suddenly laid off late into her career due to budget cuts. For the first time in years she found herself bored at home with nothing to do. She wondered if the rest of her life would feel this way: aimless, unstimulating, and resentful.

Everyone needs something to do! This aspect of retirement is one of the biggest determinants as to whether an individual thrives or flounders, and it's true for men and women, the rich and the poor alike. This chapter will discuss the reason you want to get up in the morning–because if you don't have a good reason, it's very tempting to just stay in bed. First we will go over some basic theory about fulfilling activities informed by, of all things, work psychology. Then we will explore different avenues other retirees are following to help use their time well during this exciting stage of life. By the end of this chapter, you should have some preliminary ideas of how you want to structure your days! The skies truly are the limit. I hope you are excited!

The Psychology of Work

Before examining how you want to spend your time in retirement, we first need to understand how you've spent your time in the working world. Human beings are creatures of habit, and we've spent decades of our lives developing habits around our careers. Think about your life at the height of your career: you work on certain days of the week, spend time with personal connections in the evenings, relax on your days off, and look ahead to the next vacation. Does this sound familiar? Maybe not completely, but the fact is most Americans develop a work routine of some sort. It's predictable, familiar, and, to some extent, *fulfilling*.

Entering retirement, even if we still work some, means shaking up that well-established routine. Work may not have been the most joyful reason to get out of bed in the morning, but it was an important reason nonetheless. Work plays such a strong influence on our lives. Dr. David Blustein, a psychology researcher, published a body of work in the mid-2000's summarizing the ways that working influences us. Besides structuring our time, he explained that work is also a primary means of survival, social contact, and personal accomplishment. Let's break these down because each represents an important need in our lives! And, these are needs that don't go away when we exit work and enter retirement. We need to think about ways to fulfill them, or else we run the risk of becoming depressed.

Means of Survival. This concept is self-explanatory–people work to make money, which in turn is used to pay for food, shelter, and other services we can't do without. Unless you were born with the much coveted silver spoon in your mouth, you and/or your family needed to trade in effort and time in exchange for what you need to survive. When we have saved up enough money to retire fully, then the savings become our new means of survival. Yet, as we've talked about in earlier chapters, work is increasingly becoming a component of people's retirement plans, especially in the form of part-time work. It's a good way to supplement retirement funds and help us to meet this need.

Means of Social Contact. Most jobs involve working with other people in some way. Maybe it takes the form of speaking to customers or making small-talk on the factory line. You may even have grown close friendships with the people you've worked with. It makes sense! So much time spent with the same faces, sharing the same experiences. We become accustomed to the people we interact with the most! When we leave a job, we also leave behind that required contact with others. And, if we don't set something up to replace it, then we can quickly become lonely. There are no other social things in life we are *required* to do outside of work, and so many retirees end up not seeking out social settings. It is the path of least resistance, the easiest option. Instead, many will choose to stay home, maybe watch television. It is unfortunately this very loss of social connectedness that leads many retirees to struggle once they leave work and even develop severe depression. We are, at the core, social animals.

Means of Personal Accomplishment. Our jobs, even the ones we hate, provide an undeniable means of personal accomplishment. All jobs provide you with the ability to feed your family, pay for your housing, and even buy the things that you want. *You* are the one paying for these things, through the sweat of your own efforts. Construction worker or doctor, secretary or CEO, it doesn't matter what the profession is: earning a paycheck is something to be proud of. By paying for the means of survival, we in turn are able to enjoy things in life. It is *because* you put your time in at the office that you can devote time to your family on the weekend! Your hard work paid for that movie ticket, that article of clothing, and the food in your child's mouth. Our jobs become so intertwined with our identities that we can't get away from them. What's one of the first things a new acquaintance asks you, besides your name? *"What do you do?"* And this doesn't go away during retirement–your job before retiring is still very much a part of who you are. Ask any parent or grandparent to tell you about working at their former job, and I'm sure they will have no shortage of stories. That being said, things aren't quite the same when we retire–we run the risk of losing this sense of work identity and self-esteem. We can continue to bask in the glow of our former glories, but people need a way to feel accomplished day-to-day to sustain a happy mood over time. We need a way to feel accomplished now that the job is done.

So you see, leaving the workforce does not only signal a loss of structure and direct income from work, but it also means a loss of social connectedness and sense of ongoing accomplishment. The wise thing to do is to find alternative ways to meet those needs for when work ends. Income strategies have been covered in previous chapters, and so that leaves finding ways to create structure, social connectedness, and ongoing accomplishment. Luckily, there are many ways to build these into your schedule! And with the advent of the Internet, it has never been easier to research new things and find people who share your interests. This truly represents an opportunity to pursue your passions, try something you've always wanted to try, and be the person you want to be. In retirement, you have more time than you've likely ever had before. This can be a blessing or a curse–let's fill your day with blessings.

Exercise 7: Aspirations and Interests

Below we are going to discuss some of the most common ways that retirees have been using their time to the fullest. But before we get there, I'd like to help you clarify what you are already interested in and passionate about. This exercise is very simple: on a piece of paper, write down three things that you enjoy doing or have enjoyed in the past. Maybe you've enjoyed traveling or playing a sport. Perhaps painting has been a passion of yours. It doesn't matter how impressive or mundane you may find the three things because they are *your* three things. Once you have written them down, I want you then to record three things you would like to do in the future. They can be the same items as your previous three, or they can be completely different! Maybe you've always wanted to visit Paris or learn to play the guitar. Maybe you've always wanted to try a special food from somewhere unique. Perhaps you share interests in common with Fauja Singh and Hidekichi Miyazaki, two centenarians discussed in the Health chapter, and you would like to take up running! Older folks around the world are accomplishing so many amazing things that there are really no limits as to what we can add to a bucket list. And, if you are having difficulty coming up with items, then that is okay! Feel free to revisit the exercise once we have gone through the remainder of the chapter, which is designed to help generate ideas.

Structuring Your Time

You may have been daydreaming all through your working years about all of the freetime you will have once you leave the job behind and retire! Well, all of that freetime is not what it's cracked up to be. Having endless, unstructured lengths of freetime can lead to getting nothing done and feeling stagnant. It is good to have blocks of freetime, but it's crucial to build in things to accomplish each week. Otherwise, each day will blend into the next, until they all feel the same. While you may not like the idea of scheduling things during your hard-earned freetime, keep in mind that it is *you* who are deciding how to structure your day–not a boss, not a project deadline, but you. To fight that sense of aimlessness and stagnation, our goal here is to start scheduling some things.

You may have begun an initial draft of a schedule from our previous discussion of scheduling periods of walking. If not, that is okay! You can write activities down in a planner, or you can have more of a general plan, like saying: "I go to the store on Monday mornings." Writing it down may be more helpful for following through, so use this strategy if you choose to. What we need to do is start assigning importance to certain days and periods of the week. Maybe you go to the grocery store on a certain day, and maybe you do household chores on another. You and your family may go out to breakfast each Saturday or get takeout Friday nights. Is there a good day for lawn care? Are there days when your favorite TV shows are on? You can schedule in periods of laziness and mindless activity, but do it intentionally. Since there is no inherent, built-in schedule for retirement life, we have to create it ourselves. Think of weekly or biweekly scheduled activities as goalposts to look forward to. By knowing what is coming next, we can better appreciate our time and are more likely to follow through with our current plans.

Activities in Retirement

Scheduling chores is not going to completely fill up our time, nor is it going to necessarily help us to meet our social and accomplishment needs. The following sections are avenues retirees have followed to live more fulfilling and driven lives. While not necessarily paid, they will help you to be part of something involved and meaningful. As you read through, think about your own personal interests and resources available in your area. If you could do anything within your means, what would it be? Think about the things you are passionate about and the ways that you used to enjoy using your free time; this can be a great place to start when brainstorming what you would like to do! This is your chance to start something wonderful in your life. Having at least one activity to look forward to can add something new and exciting to your week and is just what the doctor ordered to keep the blues away.

School. I know it might sound silly to consider going back to school *after* wrapping up your career, but there are a lot of great opportunities here for retirees. Many colleges and universities open their classes to older citizens for discounted fees–even for free! Usually colleges will include this information online and can be quickly found by typing the name of the school and "senior citizen tuition" into your web search browser. There are many advantages to this kind of activity, and it really presents a unique opportunity for retirees. Not only does it cost you nothing, but class times can help structure your week and encourage interaction with others who share a similar interest. Another added bonus is that you won't be required to take tests or assignments if you do not want to, meaning you can just learn from a professional instructor for the sheer pleasure of it. And, it can offer you the chance to learn something really cool, maybe that topic you've always been interested in! Ever wanted to learn more about Ancient Egypt? Take a class! How about the stars? Sign up for an astronomy course! Do you have hopes of traveling to South America or Spain? Start taking a Spanish class! There is no limit to what you can dig into.

On top of this, most colleges and universities will also offer community or extra-curricular classes. These courses are non-academic but focus instead on helping you learn new skills, like pottery, guitar, and weaving. These courses usually involve paying a small fee but can lead to really satisfying results. Shortly after my grandfather began to take woodworking classes at his local college, every member of the family received a handmade wooden bowl for the holidays. My grandmother took up painting and decorated their home with classy landscapes. I've always thought that practicing what we learn and even making a physical product from a hobby can be such a fulfilling accomplishment. We'll talk more about hobbies later, but I wanted to start this section by highlighting university courses because it's such a hidden gem for retirees.

Hobbies. Identifying hobbies can be a great place to start when exploring options for things to do. Hobbies include everything from private pastimes to group activities and from private crafts done at home to group sporting events. Performing an Internet search for your hobby in your geographical area can help you find locations nearby that cater to said hobby or clubs of people who meet to share in their similar interests. There is a great website called "Meetup.com" that can help you find existing groups involving your favorite hobby or interest.

And, if you find that there isn't a group already available, I would strongly encourage you to start your own! You never know, there are likely others out there waiting for someone to take the initiative. As they say, "If you build it, they will come!"

Especially when it comes to more physical hobbies like basketball or swimming, many retirees may face disappointment knowing they cannot get out there and compete like they used to. As we've talked about before, it takes a lot to adjust to older age! When this is the case, I always encourage my clients to consider finding ways to help stay involved somehow with the sport. While my sciatica prevents me from getting out on the courts, I can still buy season tickets for my local sports team! What a great way to fill up your schedule for the season! There may also be a youth or little league team nearby in need of volunteers or coaches. Imagine spending three nights each week inspiring young athletes to engage in the sport you love–how awesome. While we can't always control physical changes, we can still bring our appreciation and expertise for the event to the center of the stage. It oftentimes is not the hobby itself but sharing with others that can feel so meaningful.

Travel. While not a hobby and certainly not everyone's cup of tea, traveling represents a great way for retirees to spend their time. Being able to see and experience a novel place can add variety to the calendar year, and it has never been easier to travel! Car, bus, RV, boat, and train are all options for you to use, and you don't have to travel far to find a little something different. Consider staying the night in another town or in another state just to get a feel for the area. Ocean liner cruises and even river boat cruises, which are gaining in popularity, are a great way to catch the travel bug not just because all food and accommodations are covered, but because they will allow you to get a feel for many different countries on just one trip. There are also travel guides and travel groups available that will take care of the planning for you. If you are looking for something to help fill up your time and feel the need to experience something different, then you can't go wrong with travel!

Day Clubs. As you may be aware, there are many pre-existing organizations that offer community groups and events. Local senior centers usually host a wide array of activities, including games, social groups, and outings. The local library is also a good source of social clubs, and you can usually find a calendar of events featured at the circulation desk. I know that my local library hosts community seminars about various topics like cooking and birdwatching, as well as ongoing events like a monthly creative writing group. The YMCA will often feature community leagues for more athletic interests and can be a good meeting place for walking groups, pickleball leagues, and fitness classes like yoga or Tai Chi. For those who have served in the military, you may find a ready source of comradery at a wide range of community organizations, including the Vet Center, Amvets, and the VFW. The benefits of day clubs are the fact that they are easy to participate in, are ready sources of social contact, and require very little commitment. These can be a great way to meet people because you have a common interest to talk about! You may want to try out a few different programs to see if any groups suit you.

Volunteering. Spending time with others is incredibly important for maintaining a good mood, though it is not the whole picture. There is a part of all of us that inherently wants to give back or feel part of something bigger than ourselves. Volunteering your time is one way of achieving a similar feeling of achievement and personal identity that is lost when we exit work. It helps to answer the question, "What am I now that I no longer work?" We can now say, "I'm a volunteer for ___." So many meaningful organizations are able to run because of volunteers; places that do good work for the community and the world. Habitat for Humanity helps to build and renovate homes for the less fortunate. Soup kitchens rely on volunteers to feed the hungry. The Boys and Girls Club and the Big Brother Big Sisters Program help young people to grow up feeling confident and safe. Libraries need people to restock the shelves, political candidates need people to collect donations and canvas neighborhoods, and national parks need tour guides. Trees need planting, teachers need teaching aides, and coaches need support staff. There is such a need for volunteering, and retirees have a unique opportunity to help given their available freetime.

Many volunteers speak of the sense of pride they feel from seeing the results of their work–imagine driving by the house you helped build or seeing a young person graduate that you helped to tutor. Even though volunteering is not paid work, it's worth the effort for the good feelings we get in return. Organization leaders welcome volunteers with open arms, and this means you can be choosy about where you want to volunteer and for how much time. Even places not openly advertising for volunteers will gladly accept someone interested in helping out–it just takes the small effort of putting yourself forward and asking. Volunteering also includes the added bonus of interacting with other people. As you look at your schedule, do you see any areas where you might be able to fit in time for volunteering? If so, it's worth a try to see how you like it.

Faith Communities. Similar to volunteering in general, faith communities always have opportunities for people to contribute and become more involved. As non-profit organizations, religions rely heavily on members of the congregation to contribute time and re-sources. If you are part of a church, synagogue, temple, mosque, or otherwise, consider approaching the leadership of the group and asking if there is any way you can help. Most religious organizations need help with providing worship services, daycare, and organizational tasks. You can likely find a list at your place of worship of volunteering opportunities available. Faith groups are, as a whole, very welcoming and appreciative, and performing "good works" can help with growing closer to your faith. Faith communities also tend to provide many recurring events that you can join, such as study groups and social meet-ups. Given the wide range of religions and denominations, this can be a great way of joining a supportive community or growing closer to your established group.

Part-Time Work. As has been mentioned earlier, working at a part-time level is becoming increasingly more common for retirees. While the added benefit of supplemental income is the main draw, it also can benefit retirees by helping them to maintain structure, social contact, and sense of accomplishment. Think of how much you would enjoy your job if you could work at a more relaxed pace! Evidence increasingly shows that people who work longer report better health, improved mood, and increased longevity. It really goes to show how accustomed we become as humans to work and how much it provides to our lives.

While some people transition from working full-time to part-time within their same career field, this doesn't have to be the case! Retiring can mean the chance to change careers completely based on what's available or what you are passionate about. Referred to as an "encore career," doing something different can be a breath of fresh air or even the fulfillment of a lifelong passion. Perhaps you have always wanted to be an artist or a writer or an instructor. Many people are able to turn their hobbies into lucrative businesses by tapping into their hidden passions. Art shows are a great venue for selling your paintings, handmade jewelry, woven bags, and more. With the advent of the

Internet, selling goods online has never been easier with websites like Etsy.com providing a platform for many independent artists to reach customers across the globe. Some retirees relish the chance to open a business, while others enjoy the chance to keep busy. If you enjoy doing something, then there is likely a way to make money from it.

Exercise 8: Scheduling One Activity

We've discussed the many benefits of structuring your time and staying busy during your retirement years. It's very easy to embrace the well-deserved freedom of this stage of life and let time quickly slip away. So for this exercise, I want to challenge you to write down at least one social activity from the sections above that you might be interested in. You don't need to have a clear and absolute idea of what that activity is going to be: simply writing "take a class" or "volunteer" is good enough to start with. Once you have at least one activity, let's find a place to fit it into your weekly schedule. Write it in and keep your calendar in a visible place, where you'll be able to see it frequently. Again, there is something motivating about writing down our goals and reminding ourselves about them from time to time. Your activity will likely take some research and planning to put into action, but for now this is a good first step. As well, feel free to include more than one activity if you feel ambitious! Regardless, pat yourself on the shoulder or hand for taking this important step!

Building New Habits Takes Time

It's worth noting that Rome wasn't built in a day, and your schedule is not going to fill up overnight. It can take time to include new activities in your routine. University and community classes only start at certain times of year, applications for volunteering need time to be processed, and you may have to try a lot of different options before you find the one that feels right. I want to point out that doing something new–anything new–is hard and takes time! The very act of trying something out is important and worth celebrating. It takes courage and planning to put yourself forward. I would keep in mind, too, that nothing is going to feel "perfect." There may be elements of the activity that don't feel right, and there may be days when you wake up and don't feel like going. That is understandable and part of being a human! It's less important in my mind to focus on the thing you are doing and more important to focus on the fact that you are doing *something*. Because it is the act of *doing* that, at its core, helps us to feel good. I often encourage my clients to shift their thinking from, "I'm not going to do it because I don't feel like it," to "If I do it, I know I'll feel more energized and good." I can speak from personal experience that I often don't want to exercise or volunteer my time, but after the experience is over I usually feel content. Sometimes the activity itself leads to good feelings! Another way of thinking about motivation is to ask yourself: "Will I regret it more if I get up and go, or will I regret it more if I don't go?" Usually when I play hooky, I inevitably regret it later.

To help get things going, start small. Filling up your entire schedule all at once can be overwhelming and, given time, can lead to burning out! Building in one or two new things a month can be a good start, and regularly checking in with yourself to see if it is too much also helps. As well, things are easier to do when we have friends or family involved. Maybe one of your children or close friends would be interested in taking a trip somewhere, or maybe you can volunteer alongside a grandchild. The lists above are certainly not all-inclusive, especially given that every area of the country is unique. Perhaps your friends or neighbors know of things to do that you don't, or maybe they're already part of a club that you could join. Retirement doesn't have to look any particular way, so find what fits well for you!

Free-Time Felecia Revisited

Let's see how Felecia has tackled her low mood and malaise since leaving her job. After her layoff, Felecia floundered at home for a couple of weeks. At first she enjoyed the time off, yet the freedom soon turned out to be not all it was cracked up to be. Since so much of her identity had been tied to her job, she felt an emptiness now that it was gone. But slowly over time, she began to build more activities into her schedule. She followed her Primary Care Provider's advice and started to walk three times a week. As well, she called up some old friends, who were more than willing to invite her to a poetry reading at the local community center. Felecia enjoyed herself immensely and began to doodle limericks on napkins and the notepad she keeps by her bed. She built another block of time into her week: going to the nearby coffee shop each morning to write poetry for an hour. As well, she overheard that the library needs volunteers to help with upcoming events. Before she knew it, Felecia had built quite the life for herself in her newfound retirement, including scheduled walks, poetry writing, volunteering, and spending time with friends. She's even excited at the prospect of reading her own poetry at an upcoming event, and she's wondering if she can fit in an international trip later this year. Though her time now looks nothing like it did while she was working, she's very glad that things turned out so well. "My retirement is what I make of it," she often says.

Summary

Overall, it's very important to find *something* to help fill your time. When people have unstructured and unlimited freetime, they tend to struggle and sink into depression. So many fresh retirees park themselves on the couch to watch television and become a permanent fixture of the living room. Don't get me wrong, enjoying TV shows is also important! But, it's also passive, solitary, and sedentary–it doesn't help us to meet the needs of structure, socializing, or personal accomplishment. Prioritizing these needs is the most effective way to ensure they get met. The good news is, there isn't a right or wrong way to spend retirement. You are the expert on *you*–no one else knows you and your preferences as well as you yourself. Use that knowledge to inform your decision-making, and take advantage of the opportunity you have before you! Life can be sadly too short–how do you want to use your time?

Check-In #6

We are nearing the end of our journey together with only one chapter to go! We've just covered how to find activities and things to do that can improve your mood and generate a sense of personal fulfillment. In other words, you have tangible steps you can follow to better enjoy your time! Let's check in now to see how you feel now about retirement. On a scale of "0" to "10," you will select which number best describes your current mood with a "0" meaning "Not at all," a "5" meaning "half and half," and a "10" meaning "Completely."

I feel down and worried when I think about retirement.

I am a _____ out of 10 at this time.

I feel confident in my ability to lead a happy and successful retirement life.

I am a _____ out of 10 at this time.

GOLDEN RULE 6: MAKE A PLAN

W e have covered *a lot* of ground throughout this book. What seems like a straightforward transition into the golden years turns out to actually be a period of many important decisions! How we manage money, health, housing, and time all makes a big difference on whether it's a period of *thriving* or mere *surviving*. This Golden Rule, "Make a Plan," covers a few last topics and then ties together all of the threads into a cohesive, personalized series of steps you can follow.

The good news is there's no absolutely right or perfect way to retire. Everyone's situation is different! We all have different preferences, access to different resources, and varied opportunities available. Practically nobody that I work with believes they have enough money for retirement, and everyone struggles to some degree at the beginning. When the glow of the retirement party fades, it seems that the real challenge begins. I bring all of this up not to discourage you but to provide hope. It is normal to flounder or feel that your expectations have been let down.

And yet people manage. Somehow, some way, human beings draw upon the resiliency that has defined our species for millenia. We adapt and thrive, whether it's the deserts of the Sahara or the sub-zero temperatures of the Antarctic. And, we accomplish these feats through learning. Our brains are constantly analyzing situations, solving problems, and figuring out ways to do it better next time. It's embedded in our design! My hope is that this book can be a source of knowledge for you. We have gone over many different ways of improving your quality of life. If you find yourself struggling, then hopefully this book can help you overcome that struggle. Or better yet, maybe this book can help you to sidestep the pitfalls altogether through a well-informed plan. We'll get to that shortly.

You owe it to yourself to enjoy the stage of life that is your retirement and not get bogged down by the pitfalls. From a psychological standpoint, this stage is reserved for a concept we call *reminiscence*. Reminiscing is the process of looking back over your life, recalling your most important memories, and figuring out what were the most meaningful parts for you. It's a review of your personal story: the relationships you've made, your accomplishments, the highs and the lows. Reminiscence begs an answer to the question, "What did it all mean to you?" It's a way of consolidating wisdom and building up your personal sense of integrity. What can you feel proud of? If your life hasn't been easy or gone the way you planned, can you define a sense of strength from that?

It's important to spend time going over the good times and the bad and to share your stories with others. If you had the privilege of being able to listen to your parents or grandparents tell stories about their lives, then you were a part of their reminiscing process. Many retirees tell me that they derive the greatest enjoyment from sitting with friends and sharing tales about "the good old days." While it hasn't been a chapter focus in itself, relationships are a running thread throughout this book. One of the greatest risks of retirement is the tendency to isolate–don't let this be you! Make an effort to spend time with people. Make new friends and cherish your lasting relationships. The world deserves to have your presence–you know facts no one else does and see the world in a unique way no one else can. Don't hide it away–there is still so much for you to give.

Form a Retirement Team

On top of social contacts, there are relationships that every retiree would do well to start building. Think of these people as your "team," and forming our retirement plan will involve identifying these individuals. Remember that we can always accomplish more together when we work as a team! These are people who bring a special knowledge base and expertise to the table and can help you to keep enjoying your retirement years for longer. Some of these professionals have been mentioned earlier, but it's worth reiterating here because of just how important it is to put such a relationship in place now (or at least soon). If you haven't already, consider searching online for professionals in your area or ask friends or family if they have any recommendations. And note: always double-check on credentials with customer reviews and the Better Business Bureau because there are many scam artists out there!

Financial Planner. I will admit: I used to cringe away from the idea of paying someone to help me manage my money. But now I am not too prideful to say that I am eating my words! A financial planner can be invaluable at any stage of your retirement journey, and a good one will help you to save way more money than any fee would cost. Many people know that financial planners will help you to find the right places to invest your money, but more importantly for retirees they also help you to withdraw your money appropriately. A financial planner will analyze the sources of your funds and tell you how to withdraw money and when in order to avoid paying higher taxes. They are able to do this by knowing the money amount limits for tax brackets and age of withdrawal for the current year. Without this support, many retirees withdraw way too much out of certain taxable accounts and risk losing precious funds to Uncle Sam. As well, they can help you to moderate how much money you withdraw each year in order to make your money last. Without such an accountability partner, it can be very tempting to withdraw too much in the early years of retirement and not have enough in the future... when costs are likely to be even more expensive!

There are many books out there that will claim to be able to teach you how to manage your own funds during retirement. Some of them may even be able to do so! But, for something as important as your livelihood, and considering the fact that your personal situation will be unique, I vouch for hiring a professional to do it for you. That being said, some advisors are more trustworthy than others! It's recommended that you look for financial advisors who are registered under the Security Exchange Commission (SEC)--such people will have a designation called a "Registered Investment Advisor," meaning they are fiduciaries and therefore required to always put *your* financial needs first. Other advisors not held to the SEC standards may use your money in risky ways to improve *their* bottom line but not yours. Very simply, ask a potential financial advisor if they would be your fiduciary and *only* use your investments as a fiduciary would. If they are unable to do so, then you will want to find someone different for your team.

Primary Care Physician (PCP). We've talked some earlier about how important your PCP is for a happy life in retirement, but it bears repeating again here. The research shows that you will enjoy life more and have fewer expenses in retirement if you keep a healthy lifestyle, and your PCP is the best person to help you do so. Not only can your PCP help monitor your body and provide treatments to maintain wellness, but they can also refer you to other specialists that can help. PCP's, especially those who work with older patients, are increasingly finding that their patients prefer a "one-stop shop" model of care and are improving their own ability to offer more as a result. Establishing yourself with a PCP is a good idea even if you are not experiencing any severe issues because if *any kind* of change were to happen, the PCP would be able to pick up on it right away. And if you find that your current provider doesn't seem to be covering your needs well enough, then consider finding someone who can. Searching for primary care providers who specialize in "Geriatrics" or who refer to themselves as "Geriatricians" will likely be good choices, as these terms refer specifically to working with older patient concerns.

Elder Law Attorney. Especially these days, it's always good to have a lawyer on your side. I don't mean hiring a lawyer on retainer, but meeting at least once with an elder law attorney will guarantee beyond a shadow of a doubt that your needs and the needs of your family will continue to be honored. While some aspects of life are honored automatically by the law, others are not and require legal documentation. For example, if you were to pass away, then all of your assets would go to your next of kin... unless you owe significant medical expenses from a freak accident or were to be sued. Or if you were to enter a nursing home for longterm care, all of the assets connected to your name would be drained to pay for your care and not to your family's needs. Or maybe a sudden infection, such as a common urinary tract infection, were to cause you to become severely confused, and you were unable to voice your preferences for medical treatment—what would you do then?

Elder law attorneys assist with estate planning, financial trusts, living wills, final wills, and more. An elder law attorney can help protect your money so that the government or collectors will be unable to make claims on it. They can help guarantee you are able to leave an inheritance for your family and can help you to specify how your assets will be distributed. They can also create a legally binding document specifying the medical situations under which you will want to receive life-sustaining treatment: from "Full Code," meaning to sustain your life under all circumstances to "Do Not Resuscitate," meaning to allow your body to follow a natural course without life-sustaining treatment; and all areas in between. You can even specify the possible conditions under which you would like to receive certain treatments like CPR and conditions under which you wouldn't. This is a wise decision because while you may believe your preferences are self-evident, you'd be surprised at how often the rest of the world isn't on the same page! Of note as well, the sooner you reach out to put these legalities in place, the better able a lawyer will be to help you, as some aspects are time-sensitive.

Surrogate Decision-Maker. A surrogate decision-maker is someone whom you trust and deem responsible to make decisions on your behalf in the event that you are unable to make the decisions yourself. This individual can be a family member or a close friend as long as they satisfy two criteria: you trust them to act according to your best interests and they are deemed competent to do so. If, during a worst-case scenario, you are so confused that you cannot think straight or are unable to speak for yourself, then your surrogate decision-maker would step in and vouch for your needs in your place. Having this team member is kind of like having insurance in that you don't want to have to use it, but you sure are grateful it is there. Oftentimes when this is not in place, a decision-maker is found for you: either a random family member or a state-appointed guardian (A.K.A., a stranger!).

There are two types of surrogate decision-makers: "Power of Attorney" (POA) and "Durable Power of Attorney" (DPOA). A POA will step up in the event that you lack capacity to make decisions then will step back once you have overcome the condition and can make decisions for yourself again. You can specify whether you want your POA to serve for medical decisions, financial decisions, or both. A POA can help pay bills and select which physical rehabilitation facility for you to go to after being cleared by the hospital, as an example. A DPOA on the other hand is a permanent decision-maker, meaning you have been deemed incapable by a judge to ever make decisions for yourself again, likely due to a severe medical condition like dementia. Hence, this "Durable" POA will make all of your medical and financial decisions for you. Usually they will be the deciding factor as to whether your needs can be met at home or if permanent nursing home placement will be required. It takes a lot of evidence to put a DPOA in place, and it is very hard to have this designation removed once it has been assigned. Obviously, you would want this to be someone you trust whole-heartedly! Oftentimes a person's POA will be the one to become their DPOA when the time is right.

Your surrogate decision-maker will need to be familiar with your living will (i.e., whether you want to be considered "Full-Code" or "Do Not Resuscitate") and other preferences you will have under different circumstances. As these preferences can change over time, some families designate a special time of year to discuss living will preferences, such as during Thanksgiving weekend. It may be an uncomfortable conversation, but it is incredibly important. Your POA will also need to make themselves available as an emergency contact on medical documentation. In order to set up a POA, speak to an elder law attorney–they can write up the official legal document.

Mental Health Therapist. For a long time, mental health concerns have been stigmatized. People have had realistic fears of being judged or discriminated against for receiving this kind of help. Nowadays, this has changed! Medical science confirms that treating your mental health is just as important as treating your physical health, and in fact the mind and body are connected in powerful ways. When we are feeling depressed or anxious, we are more likely to develop serious, life-limiting physical illnesses like heart disease and even dementia. For this reason, it is so important to seek help if you are feeling consistently down, on edge, or nervous.

If you find this is the case leading up to your retirement or during your retirement, consider meeting with a mental health provider. These professionals specialize in building skills and offering support for people going through a hard time. They also help people who are not even depressed or anxious to improve their lives, such as by setting goals for growth and building healthy habits–many of the things that this very book hopes to achieve! Struggling with the blues? This is a great place for help. Want to live a more fulfilling life? There's a place for you.

If nothing else, meeting regularly with a mental health provider can be a great, dependable form of support. Many clients enjoy working with a therapist because it is a person who is outside or unrelated to your life. Because of this, clients can feel more free to talk about their troubles, issues they have with family, and deep insecurities. The therapist will not judge you, and there is no risk to your personal life because all mental health therapists are forbidden by law to discuss sessions out in public. In fact, as therapists we are trained to not even acknowledge our patients out in public so as to prevent unwanted questions. So, you can feel secure with this team member!

Think of a mental health therapist as your own personal cheerleader, consultant, confidant, and helper who will work to protect your needs at all costs. While mental health therapy is not for everyone, or it may not be the right time, it's always nice to know where to find help. Psychologytoday.com can help you find therapists in your area who will take your insurance. Many therapists will even offer the first visit for free to help you decide if it's right for you.

Exercise 9: Identify Your Team

This one may take some time, but it is worth the effort. The goal of this exercise is to identify at least one possible name for each of the roles on your team. You don't have to contact the individuals, just write down the names of potential candidates. If you already have people for those roles, then great! Write current and potential names down for the financial planner, primary care provider, elder law attorney, surrogate decision-maker, and mental health therapist positions on your team and keep the paper somewhere safe. You never know when this tiny step of planning ahead may come in handy, especially if you find yourself in need in the future! And, if you are having trouble identifying names, then a quick Internet search within your geographical area can help. You may find that you still are not able to fill in each name; just do the best you can. This exercise is only here to help and certainly is not required.

Exercise 10: Solidify Your Plan

We have one final exercise to complete, and actually you are already done! Well, kind of, especially if you have been completing each exercise along the way. The goal of this exercise is to solidify your plan. We want to take all of the effort you have made and put it in one place. You are welcome to write this out yourself on a blank sheet of paper, or (as a final reminder) there is a free companion workbook you can print out so all of your work can be in one place. All you would need to do is go to the Internet website LifeCanBeGolden.com and sign up for the emailing list on the homepage. Once you enter your email address, you will receive an instant response in your email inbox with the free digital workbook. As well, entering your email address will also allow you to receive updates about future books relevant to retirement life. If you've enjoyed this book, signing up for the email list would be a great way to stay informed of future publications in the series!

What you will want to do for this exercise is to write out your response to each of the following prompts. This way, all of your personalized information and goals for retirement will be in one place. Feel free to add more or skip over parts–this is *your* plan!

1. These are my personal strengths, based on challenges I've overcome in the past:

2. These are my personal goals for retirement:

3. This is my total projected yearly retirement expenses:

4. This is my total projected yearly retirement income:

5. These are my most important expenses that I will make sure to prioritize:

6. This is my preferred form of exercising and when I intend to do it each week:

7. These are the most important factors in deciding where I am going to live:

8. If I could no longer live in my current residence, here is where I would go:

9. These are things I have always been interested in and would make for fun activities:

10. This is at least one activity I would like to make time for and schedule into my retirement:

11. This is the name of a financial planner I can reach out to if needed:

12. This is the name of my primary care provider (PCP):

13. This is the name of an elder law attorney I can reach out to if needed:

14. This is the name of my preferred surrogate decision-maker:

15. This is the name of a mental health therapist I can reach out to if needed:

And there we have it! We have summarized the work you have accomplished throughout this book into a personalized plan for your retirement life! Though no one can predict the future, hopefully having a copy of this plan will help deal with issues as they come up and lead you in a positive direction. You truly have taken steps toward turning retirement into a golden opportunity; one in which you can pursue what is truly important to you. Give yourself a final pat on the shoulder or hand... No, better yet give yourself a round of applause! You have accomplished a lot and have made an investment toward your future happiness. Well done!

Check-In #7

This marks the final check-in! Now that we have a better understanding of the retirement variables of finances, health, living situation, and activities all wrapped together into a personalized plan, let's see how you feel now about retirement. On a scale of "0" to "10," you will select which number best describes your current mood with a "0" meaning "Not at all," a "5" meaning "half and half," and a "10" meaning "Completely."

I feel down and worried when I think about retirement.

I am a _____ out of 10 at this time.

I feel confident in my ability to lead a happy and successful retirement life.

I am a _____ out of 10 at this time.

Future Directions

Well, we have reached the end of our journey. Well done, you have worked through a lot of information! Hopefully you found this to be helpful and now feel more prepared for retirement. If not, hopefully that means you were already feeling in good shape, and so this book can provide you with peace of mind. It's also possible that you feel worse than when you started—sometimes developing a greater understanding of a problem can cause us to feel *more* overwhelmed and even *less* prepared than we originally thought! For many, feeling worse off may be the result of one or two sticking points, such as finances or concern about where to live. If that is the case, I encourage you to re-read the Golden Rule that covers that topic while paying special attention to the options and strategies described. If you are still feeling lost or hopeless, then this may be the perfect opportunity for a little extra help. Consider reaching out to the mental health therapist you identified within your plan for help working through the problem. Even if the therapist doesn't specialize in retirement issues, the tools they can teach you in person will be helpful for overcoming the problem. Sometimes a different perspective can be just what the doctor ordered. And remember, you've identified past obstacles that you were able to overcome—I'm sure those challenges were not easy at first! You are a creative and resilient person, and retirement is in many ways similar to other transitions you've made in the past. Stay focused and I'm sure things will get better!

Remember that while retirement comes with its challenges, it also is an opportunity for growth and adventure. Even if you struggle, I am sure that you will do great if you stick with it. Please do not forget that there is always help available, and there are always opportunities to provide help to others in turn.

I hope you've enjoyed this book! I am passionate about helping others to succeed, and so my goal is to continue writing books. Lord willing, you will soon see more Golden Rule books coming out on other important topics specific to older individuals. Stay tuned for upcoming books in this series, including:

Life Satisfaction

Nursing Homes

Living with Dementia

Caregiving

Grief

Relationships

Mental Health

Women's Health

...And more!

Again, if you'd like to stay up to date on these future projects, please consider stopping by LifeCanBeGolden.com and signing up for the email list. I will provide updates over time on future books, including pre-release sales and other helpful resources. It is absolutely free to sign up.

And, if you found this book to be helpful, feel free to leave a review on Amazon.com or Goodreads.com; or, consider recommending it to a friend! My hope is to spread the information in this book to as many people as possible. We're in this together!

RESEARCH CITATIONS

The following sources were cited in this book:

Adams, G. A., & Rau, B. L. (2011). Putting off tomorrow to do what you want today: Planning for retirement. *American Psychologist, 66*(3), 180–192.

Baxter, S., Blank, L., Cantrell, A. *et al.* Is working in later life good for your health? A systematic review of health outcomes resulting from extended working lives. *BMC Public Health* 21, 1356 (2021). https://doi.org/10.1186/s12889-021-11423-2

Blustein, D. L. (2006). *The psychology of working: A new perspective for career development, counseling, and public policy.* Lawrence Erlbaum Associates Publishers.

Chidambaram, P. (2022). A Look at Nursing Facility Characteristics Through July 2022. *Kaiser Family Foundation.* https://www.kff.org/medicaid/issue-brief/a-look-at-nursing-facility-characteristics-through-july-2022/

Han, BH, Brennan, JJ, Orozco, MA, Moore, AA, Castillo, EM. Trends in emergency department visits associated with cannabis use among older adults in California, 2005–2019. *J Am Geriatr Soc.* 2023; 71(4): 1267- 1274. doi:

Markowitz, A. (2023). Top five states where retirees are moving. *AARP.* https://www.aarp.org/retirement/planning-for-retirement/info-2023/most-popular-relocation-states

National Institute on Aging. (2021). Depression and older adults. https://www.nia.nih.gov/health/depression-and-older-adults

National Institutes of Health. NIH.org

Penn, L. T., & Lent, R. W. (2021). Retiring or rewiring? Test of a social cognitive model of retirement planning. *Journal of Counseling Psychology, 68*(5), 538–549. https://doi.org/10.1037/cou0000530

Top Countries. (2023) *International Living.* https://internationalliving.com/country/

ACKNOWLEDGEMENTS

I could not have finished this work without the help of my own support system. I've first been guided by great researchers, both directly and through reading their published studies. My mentor and advisor, Dr. Bob Lent, was pivotal in my own development as a researcher. As well, the research studies of David Blustein, Gary Adams, and Barbara Rau were highly influential in my own work. My geropsychology clinical mentors, including Dr.'s Carrie Ambrose, Timothy Ketterson, Julius Gylys, Kevin Lancer, Carly Ostrum, Anne Mueller, Elizabeth Hirschhorn, and Douglas Lane, also helped shape who I am as a clinician both through their example and through their unique ways of putting complicated concepts into words. I'd also like to thank GuideStar Eldercare for giving me the chance to work with patients in nursing homes and my colleagues at Spalding University for providing me with the support to continue researching and mentoring future psychologists. As well, I want to thank all of my patients; it has been a pleasure working with you, and please know that *I* have learned so much from our time together.

Lastly, I'd like to thank my friends and family. Your support has meant so much to me–this and other projects like it would have fallen by the wayside if not for you. Thank you to my best friends Ariel, Matt, and Justin for cheering me on. Thank you to my mother, Barbara, and my mother-in-law, Tammy, for helping in so many different ways. And most of all thank you to my wife, Amber, and our son, George–without you, none of this would be possible.

Sneak Peak: The Golden Rule of Life Satisfaction

B elow you will find the first few pages from the next book in the Golden Rules Series: *The Golden Rules of Life Satisfaction.* Sign up for the email list at *LifeCanBeGolden.com* for updates on the future release date and sales!

Well done! By opening this book, you have taken the first step toward bettering your overall well-being, even in old age. Maybe you find yourself frequently struggling to find motivation or even get up out of bed in the morning. Perhaps it feels like you have no direction, that life seems tasteless or flat. Or, you might feel overall content most of the time and are looking for ways to grow and feel even better. If any of the above applies to you, then I grant you a hearty welcome! We'll use the following chapters, styled as "The Golden Rules of Life Satisfaction," to learn more about mood and discuss strategies to feel more fulfilled each day. I'm so excited to work with you!

Let's talk about what I mean by "fulfilled," as it is going to be the main goal of this book. To feel fulfilled means having enough of everything you need. You have something to look forward to each day, and your time feels meaningful. You may not feel *happy* every second of the day (This is impossible!), but you find moments of happiness, pockets of joy throughout the day. Unlike happiness which is fleeting, a sense of fulfillment stays with you for the long term. And, it's never too late in life to make this a reality.

Imagine for a moment this possible future: you wake up in the morning, and you feel *energized.* You feel a sense of *calm* and *relaxation.* At the same time, there's a tickle of anticipation because there are *things you are looking forward to* later in the day. Perhaps things that involve the *people you care about* or maybe *things that make you feel fulfilled on your own.* You have *positive thoughts* and you feel a healthy sense of *pride for who you are.* You know that little things are going to come up and bother you, but they are so unimportant compared to your overall *life satisfaction.* You feel ready to grab a cup of coffee or tea and start your day.

If this description appeals to you, then I am so glad you have picked up this book! Helping people to achieve such a life is what makes me feel fulfilled–let's help you to get there!

This book is written with any style of person in mind. Everyone feels down sometimes! Blue, down in the dumps, in a rut, low-down. Your get-up-and-go just got up and went. Everything just feels kind of gray and *blah.* Most of the time, this low feeling is temporary and won't last for longer than a day, maybe two. This is natural and part of being human. You really can't get through life without feeling down some of the time–otherwise, we wouldn't know what feeling "good" means! Nevertheless, it's never an enjoyable experience to feel down, and we often want to make the experience as brief and painless as possible and replace it with feeling fulfilled.

When our low mood persists for many days in a row, we in the health profession become concerned about depression. This persisting low mood may feel like a minor inconvenience or a debilitating illness. When I imagine severe de*pression*, I conjure up the vision of a giant weight actually *pressing down* onto a person's back. The weight is so heavy that their chest, arms, and legs are all trapped, pushed deep into the hard ground. The person can't lift a finger, and they've lost the motivation to do so. Even raising their nose up to breathe feels like it takes a great effort. The person is completely flattened, helpless, and stuck. When this happens, my goal as a mental health therapist is to help get that person "unstuck" as quickly as possible and stay free of the giant weight.

This can be easier said than done, and the challenge of overcoming depression is often unique for older individuals. There are many reasons why this is so!

...Stay tuned for more!

ABOUT THE AUTHOR

D r. Lee Penn, PhD, is a psychologist with over a decade working with hundreds of patients in the later stages of life. He has worked in a variety of settings, including the Veterans Affairs administration, nursing homes, private practice offices, and academic departments. Currently he is a professor at Spalding University, where he teaches future psychologists and furthers his research into matters affecting older individuals. Learn more about his work, free supplemental materials, and upcoming books in the Golden Rules series at his website: LifeCanBeGolden.com.

Made in the USA
Las Vegas, NV
25 June 2024

91462718R00083